Making It in Corporate America

MAKING IT IN CORPORATE AMERICA

How Women Can Survive, Prosper, and Make a Difference

Diane Smallen-Grob

Westport, Connecticut
London

Library of Congress Cataloging-in-Publication Data

Smallen-Grob, Diane.
  Making it in corporate America: how women can survive, prosper, and make a difference / Diane Smallen-Grob.
    p. cm.
  Includes bibliographical references and index.
  ISBN 0–275–98110–X
    1. Women executives—United States. I. Title.
  HD6054.4.U6S6 2003
  658.4′09′082—dc21   2003048206

British Library Cataloguing in Publication Data is available.

Library of Congress Catalog Card Number: 2003048206
ISBN: 0–275–98110–X

First published in 2003

Praeger Publishers, 88 Post Road West, Westport, CT 06881
An imprint of Greenwood Publishing Group, Inc.
www.praeger.com

Printed in the United States of America

The paper used in this book complies with the Permanent Paper Standard issued by the National Information Standards Organization (Z39.48–1984).

10 9 8 7 6 5 4 3 2 1

To Werner, with whom nothing is impossible.

CONTENTS

ACKNOWLEDGMENTS

I couldn't walk away from years in business and leave all the unanswered questions asked by my youngest and most promising starlets. Therefore, I thank Stephanie Hoeckle and Monica Goldstein for asking me to tell them what they needed to know and for hoping I could give them all the answers. This book is written for them. I am indebted to my husband for being my light, my spirit, and my support and to Karen Gottlieb for reading the manuscript, to Peggy Hutson and Marie Ellen Larcada for having faith in me. I shelved this book after September 11, 2001, thinking women and corporations were so meaningless during that time of tragedy. It all seemed irrelevant. But the world came back and with it all the same issues, including women's place in the executive suite.

I could not have even conceived writing this book without the help of all the wonderful women I interviewed. For those named and those who preferred to remain anonymous I am eternally grateful. They gave me their time and candor. I am honored to have met them all and to be able to pass on their magnificent advice to younger generations. I thank all the people who cheered me on and introduced me to the women I had never met before, especially Lois Oppenheim and Penelope Dixon.

Most of all, I hope this is the last book that ever has to be written on this subject.

INTRODUCTION: FIRST STEPS

Tell me and I forget. Show me and I remember. Involve me and I understand.

—Chinese Proverb

To date, the best advice about making it as a woman in a man's world comes from Eleanor Roosevelt, probably the greatest role model for all of us. Although her remarks were targeted at surviving public life in Washington, D.C., these words apply to any woman leaving the sanctity of her home to make it in a bigger place, wherever and whatever that place may be. In her words:

You cannot take anything personally.
You cannot bear grudges.
You must finish the day's work when the day's work is done.
You cannot get discouraged too easily.
You have to take defeat over and over again and pick up and go on.
Be sure of your facts.
Argue the other side with a friend until you have found the answer to every point which might be brought up against you.
Women who are willing to be leaders must stand out and be shot at. More and more they are going to do it, and more and more they should do it.
Every woman in public life needs to develop skin as tough as rhinoceros hide.[1]

Eleanor Roosevelt's advice is unassailable. Making it in the business world is not rocket science. We couldn't do much better than her nine suggestions even if we combine all the how-to books, all the advice, all the magazine articles written for us. Just as there are millions being made writing diet books, there are hundreds of books giving us five ways to win at a man's game. And just as losing weight does not become easier if we spend more money on tapes, books, and magic potions, reading books on adopting male stratagems won't open the doors to the board-room for women. Succeeding as a woman in business follows a simple recipe, seasoned with some serendipity.

Fundamentally, we face only a few scenarios in the workplace. How we react to them shouldn't change all that much over time. We have learned a tremendous amount about the skills and behavior necessary to get the next promotion. Fortunately, the men we work with have learned a lot, too, and are getting used to seeing us in the office next door. Perhaps they learned to accept women in the work world under duress, perhaps it was legislated at company headquarters, or perhaps mothers, wives, sisters, or daughters brought them up well. The good news is that more men are sensitive and aware now than ever before.

Is this the end of the story? Have women come the long way we have been convinced we have? Well, yes and no. For sure, many more of us are working, and working in more senior positions. As it should be. But the percentages at the top are still unimpressive.

Where are we, the first generation, the women early baby boomers (WEBBs) now, thirty to thirty-five years after graduating from college? Given our age, experience, and education, we should be right up there on the executive floors of corporate America. Were it so, there might be fewer scandals and richer shareholders.

Plenty of solid statistics that we all need to know are shared in this book. But more important, we women in corporations have our own stories, the real-life experiences we have endured and used to toughen our hides. Perhaps these stories can provide what a role model would as you work your way through the corporate maze. I learned a lot research-ing and writing this book. I only wish I had known then what I have learned now.

For all the advice books written on success, on making it as women in a man's world, or on getting power, there are more real stories by women in top positions who did it their way. Their way worked quite well. And although all the women with whom I spoke took different paths to their success, they shared similar personality traits, similar luck, but most important, they all demonstrated confidence in making the choices they made.

Men have it easier. Maybe not as interesting, but easier. They don't have to make life changing choices at every step. From the start, most men get on a course that veers very little. Few men choose middle management as a goal, even if that is as far as they get.

Some days there is a convergence of so much information that it forces you to reflect about the worth of our achievements. Besides Catalyst, the "nonprofit research and advisory organization working to advance women in business," dozens of think tanks are studying women in the workforce. Each study approaches our situation from a new angle. They look at why we get ahead and why we don't get ahead. The most compelling and disquieting concern, however, is that we women do serious harm to ourselves perhaps more than men have done. Call it the "betrayal of women," "women vs. women," whatever. It is serious, it is powerful, and it is the one reason we refight the same battles for centuries. Men may use their sheer physical power and strength to defeat us, but we inflict mental warfare on ourselves. Either way, we end up losing.

So where are we? Not that much further along than where we were. Little has changed. Much of what we have done has actually had little effect. In fact, if we compared our goals during the heady days of the feminist revolution to our results, a strict statistician might say we failed. In 1959, we earned a little more than fifty cents to the dollar a man earned. Forty-two years later we earn seventy-two cents for the same work. A gain of a little bit more than one cent per year. We stay at about three to five CEOs in the Fortune 500.

Maybe our priorities have changed and our goals are not as lofty today. Maybe we are ready to celebrate "lady chic," as Maureen Dowd suggests. Maybe it is true that today's women "want to be rescued . . . want to shop till they drop . . . want to get married and stay home and be taken care of." That we don't earn it all ourselves is not a concern any longer. "Thirty-five years of striving have tuckered women out. 'You go girl!' has downshifted to 'You go lie down, girl.' "[2] The final say is that with all we WEBBs did, all we strived for, and all the blood, sweat, and buckets of tears, we have not accomplished what we set out to accomplish. We have hardly made a dent in the very top echelons of corporate management, and we haven't been successful pied pipers. Young women today, graduate degrees in hand, don't think they will find their nirvana in business. And as long as we don't swell the middle management ranks, we won't see the top.

WEBBs failed simply because all things being equal, we didn't always believe in ourselves. It seemed like we did, but too many of us were dogged by a lack of self-confidence, and a lack of sisterly or team support. At some point, we showed our vulnerability. It wasn't easy to stay in there and fight. Too many of us walked away too soon. We didn't use all that we had.

Games Mother Never Taught You and *The Managerial Woman*[3] are the books WEBBs were told to read. Those were the books on my MBA reading list. And those were the advice books that most of the women I spoke with also remembered. Women's issues and rights were not huge in those days. We were, a decade later, closer to riding the crest of the second wave of feminism.

Did all this matter for the WEBBs who stayed in the game for the long run? Many of the women I spoke with had just about burned out. It is not as if they want to quit, but they seek new, different types of challenges. One day, they decide it is no longer worth replaying the myth of Sisyphus.

But we are all still wheels turning in space. What about the others who are still there, running corporations or divisions of large corporations? What helped them get there? What are the major peeves that have to be ignored, filed away? It is doubtful that drive and ambition were the only motivating forces that propelled them and us. This book is about all that.

And what is the simple process suggested in my first paragraph? How can we synthesize and extrapolate what a role model would have shown us—to understand both the macro and the micro issues, to capture the essence of a simple process? I devised a list of questions to guide each interview.

I wanted answers from women in business, at all executive levels. Since WEBBs didn't have role models, we had to create our own. I hope our legacy will ease the way for this generation's young women choosing business as their career track. Reading the stories of the women in the book should provide serious food for thought for young women today. And if they really get it, they will understand the power of working together for their greater good.

NOTES

1. From Blanche Wiesen Cook, *Eleanor Roosevelt. Volume 2: 1933–1938* (New York: Viking, 1999); also quoted in Maureen Dowd, *E.R., New York Times,* July 4, 1999, book review section.

2. Maureen Dowd, "Rescue Me Please," *New York Times,* June 7, 2000.

3. Betty Lehan Harragan, *Games Mother Never Taught You* (New York: Warner Books, 1978); and Margaret Hennig and Anne Jardim, *The Managerial Woman* (New York: Pocket Books, 1978).

Part I

THE TWENTIETH CENTURY

Chapter 1

TWENTIETH-CENTURY MEMORIES

Women who seek to be equal with men lack ambition.
—Timothy Leary

The spring and summer of 1945 marked the end of World War II. The fall of that same year heralded the start of a revolution. During the ten years following the end of the war, the United States witnessed the birth of 18 million girls. And the postwar baby boom began.

Mothers dreamed that their daughters would grow up to marry princes. Fathers believed their little princesses were too good for most mortal men. The sons were brought up as boys always had been: to rule the roost, play good sports, get good jobs, provide for a family.

Twenty some odd years later, these children, now young men and women armed with college degrees, most in liberal arts, took to the pavements looking for work. For the boys, it was business as usual. For the girls, it was totally unusual. What to do with the girls?

I was one of those girls.

No one was prepared for the onslaught, and neither were we. We were better educated than any group of women before us. We also had more freedom. This was perplexing to our parents, to potential employers, and surely to potential older colleagues. We lacked experience, but most of all we lacked role models. For the most part our mothers didn't have careers, even those who worked.

An entire generation of women early baby boomers, or *WEBB*s, now in their late forties through late fifties, entered the workforce, at some point in their lives, unaware of what to expect or what track to take. In fact, when they looked for work after college, they found few tracks available. Typically, the only starting position being offered in corporations was that of secretary. And being a secretary did not constitute an entry-level track. It was not nearly akin to the mailroom, where a slew of male corporate leaders started. No, being a secretary was more or less a dead end. And often, it was the only position offered, no matter what educational background a woman had.

For these women, teaching was the ideal profession, as passed on from mother to daughter. The track was simple: college, marriage, teaching, motherhood, teaching. And many women set off taking that route. But growing numbers moved away from teaching, often to get graduate degrees in business, the humanities, law or medicine.

We had more than our fair share of trials and tribulations on the way to more senior positions. A brief stroll through the decades that shaped us gives today's woman a view of what we had to endure. And it wasn't always pretty. But it is worth paying attention to. Like it or not, history does repeat itself; they call it cycles. In the words of the American poet, essayist, and philosopher George Santayana, "those who cannot remember the past are condemned to repeat it."

We started out as "the Little Women." Little women as opposed to our mothers who individually were each the little woman. We had no plans or career aspirations, nor were we supposed to.

Our journey began in the 1940s, the birth decade for the first half of the first generation of WEBBs. During World War II, our mothers were hailed as the saviors of American business. They did it all. From factory worker to supervisor, our moms managed the whole business. All the Rosie the Riveters provided the support, the materiel, and the uniforms for their men on the front. As a tribute, Wonder Woman was introduced in 1941. The day the war ended so did their competence. Women were laid off in amazingly large numbers—even before they became pregnant and created the great American baby boom.

World War II also created the male dominance force. Boys in uniform became men overnight. Young kids went through basic training and immediately overseas to fight in a war where face-to-face combat was constant. And they bonded. They shared a very deep experience. When the war ended, mothers, wives, and girlfriends could rarely penetrate this bond or understand what these boys—now men—went through. Men established "old boy networks" even before they became old boys. If you were a sergeant in the army, you maintained a certain rank in civilian life. For WACs (Women's Army Corps) it wasn't the same.

Our fathers, many of whom had grown up during World War II, saw their little princesses as wives and mothers, not as business colleagues. They were not comfortable imagining us as "one of the guys."

To change their comfort zone was not tenable. They were not going to hire us for those management trainee spots no matter how much we could contribute, how smart we were, or even how well we could manage a career track. The men who were hiring us measured their own success as husbands and fathers by the fact that their wives did not have to work. So the women the male executive worked with or hired were considered inferior to his own wife, or not to be taken totally seriously, like his daughter.

We were good girls, too. We were brought up to be good girls. Seen, not heard, smiles, not frowns. "Fresh" was not an admirable trait. Modesty was always the best policy. Tooting our own horn was unacceptable. If we were good, someone would find out soon enough. Life was a constant trade-off in gratification. Whatever you wanted now would be better later. You were told to wait until you were grown up, graduated, married, or a parent to get what you wanted. You saved for a rainy day because that was what your parents did, something they had learned from their own parents during the Depression. Living in a well-hidden tiny crevice of your soul was Mom's (and Grandma's) admonition that you shouldn't be too smart or too independent or too capable. Because then why would you need a man? Everything in moderation.

Just in time for us, Congress passed the Civil Rights Act of 1964. Title VII of the Civil Rights Act prohibited all forms of discrimination in the workplace. That included discrimination against women and blacks.

Prior to Title VII, there were no entry-level jobs targeted to women, unless you consider secretary as entry level. Most businesses did just that. Even after we longed for the exciting job, the yet unnamed profession, almost everything we were offered was secretarial. They gave the job many interesting names like executive assistant, specialist, gal Friday. Ultimately, being a secretary was our foot in the door.

The passage of the Civil Rights Act helped spawn the 1970s movement that became known as feminism. Regrettably for the movement as a whole, many of the more adamant, militaristic believers engendered fear in both men and women alike. Men were scared about change in their comfort zone, an end to the old boys' game.

By the mere fact of adding a clause—Title VII—ensuring no discrimination against color, creed, or sex, we women believed that, by law, corporate doors would be wide open to us. It just seemed natural then that all of us WEBBs entering the workforce would be allowed on the same tracks as the men or boys (at that age) who were also starting out.

Just what did Title VII promise us? And when were the deliverables supposed to be rendered? Surely not in 1964, or 1966, or 1968 when I looked for my first job. I doubt I would have noticed a difference. I do remember that each time I went for an interview, either through an employment agency or directly with a company, I had to take a typing test. I was even tested on how fast I wrote since I didn't take shorthand. Every woman I knew had to do the same. And we never thought there was anything odd about it. "A summa cum laude graduate and all the jobs I was offered, remember this is 1973, were basically typing jobs, or assistant for somebody in advertising. All typing jobs, in effect," lamented Judy Schneider, now president and chief executive officer of her own company, The BPI Group Inc.

The newspaper ads even separated the job offerings by "male wanted" and "female wanted"; the college grad sections were subdivided into male/female as well. And companies were allowed to ask us anything they wanted: about marriage, thoughts of future marriage, children. Chickie Bucco, vice president and director of marketing sales at KTVG Direct Marketing, was told she couldn't sell because women couldn't do that. When Title VII began to kick in, men interviewers, feeling the pressure to hire women, still asked peculiar questions such as "When was the last time you cried?"

Management trainee calls were never passed on to women; they were for men only. We were offered "gal Friday" positions instead, admin positions (under the college grad rubric though). If we tried to go for a better position, we were told we couldn't do it because we had no experience. The guys who graduated with us were held to a different standard. Miraculously, they didn't need prior experience. It was assumed, although not usually stated, that women were only going to work until we got married or perhaps until we had children. There was no long term for us. Judy Schneider, of The BPI Group, told me that a few years after she had obtained her MBA from Columbia and had completed a training program at Bankers' Trust, she joined Seagram's: "I was the first woman that the treasurer's department had ever hired as a financial analyst. But I was told I would never be an assistant treasurer because I was a female. They told me straight out."

Years later, as an offshoot to Title VII, a lot of noise was made about creating Equal Employment Opportunity (EEO) departments within medium to large corporations. These departments were supposed to protect us all—women, blacks, Hispanics—from undue discrimination on the job. For the most part, however, the women that businesses put into these positions seemed to have been selected precisely because they toed the company line. These began as powerless positions that in truth protected no one.

The creation of the Equal Employment Opportunity Commission (EEOC) was intended to stop the discrimination that was so rampant in business. But the catch was it meant our word against the company's. Establishing such a department meant that the company had to bend over backward to demonstrate its integrity. If you were gutsy enough to approach the EEO department, because it represented you in your company, or if you contacted the EEOC directly, you had to present an airtight case. The receptionist in your EEO company department had to believe you for you to even get in the door. The last thing the department wanted was to push through a case that wasn't a totally blatant act of discrimination.

By the 1980s, the discrimination was far subtler. We knew something was wrong. So many years of making us believe that we just didn't have what it takes to make it in business rubbed off and that was what we ended up believing. Many women got turned off and walked away. Many others were laid off during slower times in the 1980s recession and never returned. Business would have been a lot better with more women there.

In May 2000, President Clinton signed an equal pay amendment to the Equal Rights Amendment (ERA). Fighting to pass the ERA in full, and in part, had been going on for more than thirty years. Other than a blip in the news, there was no follow-up and little expected consequence. The first equal rights amendment was introduced in Congress in 1923, three years after women won the right to vote. It has been introduced in Congress every session since then. Eighty years ago. And for all this time, the measure has been introduced, ratified, overturned, upheld. Ratified by Congress, in 1972, the amendment was then given a date seven years hence to get ratification by all fifty states. This date was extended several times over the following three years. By 1980, however, the Republican Party reversed the support it had given the amendment since its inception. This was the year Ronald Reagan was elected president on the Republican ticket. This was the decade WEBBs were entering the business world with education, some experience, and a lot of ambition. This was the beginning of the backlash.

Socrates wrote that "Once made equal to man, woman becomes his superior." That was the apprehension in Congress in its continual reversal for support of ratification. The ERA would take Title VII of the Civil Rights amendment one step further:

Equal Rights Amendment

Section 1. Equality of Rights under the law shall not be denied or abridged by the United States or any state on account of sex.

Section 2. The Congress shall have the power to enforce, by appropriate legislation, the provisions of this article.

Section 3. This amendment shall take effect two years after the date of ratification.

Supporters contend that the ERA is needed because the equal protection clause of the Fourteenth Amendment does not provide adequate protection against sex discrimination. Opponents claim that the ERA will provide no benefits and may hurt women. We'll take our chances.

One of the fears instigated by the ERA is that "women libbers" would take over, consequently harming our laws and our families. This argument was a precursor to "family values." Today, without espousing a movement, women seek common ground to legislate backing within our laws and constitution.

Espousing women's lib as a way of life, for example, was not practical for us in the 1970s or 1980s. We had so many other issues to deal with in our daily work life. And there was something uncomfortable for us in women's lib. It was asking us to give up too much at one time, more than we were comfortable doing.

But if it wasn't women's lib, our WEBB generation was still a generation of causes. Everyone I knew was marching for or against something: against the Vietnam War, for civil rights, for the end of college core requirements, for women's rights. The list grew as we did. No one could call our generation apathetic. "We wore dresses and skirts all the way we fought in high school to wear slacks. We graduated high school, we were virgins, we fought for liberation, we fought for birth control, we fought to go on to graduate school, and we fought for abortion, for divorce. We fought for all those things. We were the generation to pave the way but we were not raised for that; we were raised to get married," agreed Judy.

We wanted to create meaningful lives. We wanted to own our own pocketbooks. If we earned our own living, then we could do what we wanted and buy what we wanted and live like we wanted to and with whom. We wanted our independence and never really thought it would be mutually exclusive of other things we also wanted, like marriage and children. I don't believe it occurred to any of us that we were making exclusionary choices. Or even declarations stating our "super woman-ness."

We thought we had the world by the balls and all the time we'd ever need.

By the 1990s, we found ourselves stuck between men who didn't fully accept our new authority, and the women who dismissed us precisely for the path we paved for them. And we found ourselves unmarried or married but without children and wondering how the hell that happened. Our choices were made or made for us. Time never seemed pressing, and although there was always knowledge of the biological clock, we really didn't think it was *ours*.

That old biological clock threat—if the meanness and isolation didn't get us to quit, fears about the losing time on that clock were sure to get a rise out of us. Of course we were scared. Were the choices we were making then going to change our lives forever? Yes. And they did.[1]

The incredible bull market starting in 1984 didn't make Wall Street any kinder to women. There were always exceptions, and there were always extraordinary women joining Street firms. But during the Reagan presidency and the inception of the market boom, other messages were being conveyed. These firms did not hang out the welcome sign to women. If anything, the wealth that was being created hardened the stance these firms had. Whereas exceptions were often made for men who knew someone who knew someone, the same bonhomie was rarely extended to women.

During those years, overall complaints to the EEOC (for all businesses) increased by 25 percent, according to Susan Faludi in her book *Backlash*. Specific "complaints of exclusion, demotions and discharges on the basis of sex soared by 30 percent."[2] And these are the ones we know about. More complaints were actually made to the EEOC but were tossed out along the way.

The last milestone in our career track came in 1991. By that year, the "glass ceiling" was an accepted fact, so much so that President George H. Bush appointed a twenty-one-member bipartisan commission, appropriately called the Federal Glass Ceiling Commission. The commission, created by the Civil Rights Act of 1991, was approved by congressional leaders, and chaired by the secretary of labor.

The assignment was to study what the commission called "artificial barriers to the advancement of minority men and all women into management and decision-making positions in Corporate America"[3] and to submit their findings and recommendations, in writing, to the president and to appropriate congressional committees. The Federal Glass Ceiling Commission gathered information about all the targeted groups by investigating their preparedness and available opportunities, as well as current management practices. They compared industries where women and minorities were promoted versus those where they were not.

The commission held hearings throughout the country, conducted a myriad of focus groups, and thoroughly combed through and reported on analyses of special U.S. Census Bureau data. What they learned indeed confirmed the existence of a glass ceiling that excluded both women and minorities from the highest levels of management. They concluded that the prejudice, which existed against both minorities and white women, was the single most important barrier for their advancement to the executive ranks. Commission members found, in the studies they analyzed, that CEOs and top executives did understand the value of diversity to both the profitability and growth of their business. They just did not do anything about it. The commission theorized, therefore, that the movement toward a more diverse enterprise was at best slow.

The commission's findings were certainly not news to the tens of thousands of WEBBs in the workforce. We were hindered by the following: a lack of management training; inhospitable corporate climates; numerous barriers leading to the token woman job syndrome; lack of career track positions, which meant few if any women in top positions for the upcoming decade; fewer opportunities for career development or additional training tailored to getting those top positions; different standards for performance evaluations (hardly any woman I know has not mentioned this as hurtful to her career at some point); behavior unbecoming a gentleman, but not unbecoming a good ol' boy, sure of his position, on the right track and scared about being surpassed by a woman; and, last, the lack of mentoring.

The government was guilty of not enforcing laws to protect both women and minorities. And to overcome that situation, it attempted to suggest, as well as legislate, behavior that in a perfect world might have accomplished the assignment. But in the real world, we all realized how tough it was to legislate against habits and learned behaviors that began in kindergarten. Psychologically, men were not ready then, and may not be now, for women to move ahead as quickly, as successfully, as they ought to given their education and natural abilities.

Both corporate and government advisers understood that any change had to come from the top of the corporation. In fact, change rests with the policies and strategies from the CEO downward, which determined then, as it does now, the corporate climate. Knowing that, it is easy to identify the policies Xerox followed in hiring women and minorities as compared with GE, where the former CEO was revered globally for his management style and practice yet no woman and only one black made it to a position near the top.

It takes at least a decade to see any sort of difference in the makeup of management. That means we need to understand the percentage of women in management training positions today to forecast what the executive suite will look like after 2010. We find a considerable increase from twenty years ago when the WEBBs entered the workplace. What we don't know is when the equation will equalize to the extent where the CEO pool is representative of the true balance of women in the business world. There was in increase of one percentage point of women in full-time wage and salary positions from 2000 to 2001. That means that there were 47.1 percent of women in executive, administrative, and managerial occupations, according to Bureau of Labor Statistics numbers.[4] That's a lot of working women. Yet, as I note in Chapter 12, the increases in corporate officer positions and top earners are still excruciatingly small. Our participation on corporate boards is almost static at about 12 percent.[5] We do move upward, but the movement is still painfully slow.

What this also means is that statistically, if we expect to see more women CEOs in the next few years, we should be well ensconced today in the most senior positions. We're not. Even skipping the generation that follows the WEBBs and going directly to Gen Xers, we still don't have the full presence needed to start filling those CEO slots because we drop out in incrementally large numbers for personal and professional reasons. Mary Barneby, president, Delaware Retail Investment Services, agreed:

> From an experience and educational standpoint there should be more at the top. But many of us just said, I'm tired. I'm tired of carrying this burden of being a role model and perhaps it is time not to play the politics anymore and move off and do something else. I don't really know what we are thinking. I still feel very much like it is my responsibility and am not sure about what younger people are thinking about now.
>
> There is this kind of lack for the development of people that exists right now. You come in, you're an A player, you produce and if you're not there on the right day, we are not going to give you the tools, we don't have the time.

Many corporate and government initiatives did result from the commission's report, including mandates and internal corporate mentoring programs. The concerns were not just about the hiring of women and minorities but, more important, about their progression into higher management and decision-making positions. We know that so many of these women, as well as minorities, were very well educated. They were recruited from some of the country's best graduate and MBA programs. Their progression, however, was not on a par with their credentials.

The initial action plan was to determine the extent to which women and minorities were discriminated against; the second was to present a report to Congress in the summer of 1995 detailing the recommendations in a strategic plan that aimed to dismantle these "artificial barriers to advancement." As stated in the original Federal Glass Ceiling Commission executive summary, "Emphasis is placed on perceptions because perceptions, true or not, perpetuate the existence of the glass ceiling barrier."[6]

Several of the internal structural barriers are very familiar to our universe today: lack of mentoring, training, and opportunities for career development. WEBBs can tell you that, as women, we were placed in softer jobs, not the kind that cause us to stand out or that make CEOs or anyone in management notice our talents. We still lose out on the job assignments that emerge on the revenue-producing side of the business. We will not see the inside of any boardroom without more access to critical assignments on highly visible task forces and committees to ensure our development within the corporate structure.

Results of the research offered by the Federal Glass Ceiling Commission then, and surveys presented by the largest executive recruitment firms now, confirm the measly statistics that there are still not many of us in senior executive positions. The importance of the finding now is that the first wave of baby boomers—women who are now in their late forties through late fifties—have suffered the most in these results. These women are at exactly the age when successful businesspeople take center stage and run their companies. And that would be now.

Women in corporations today are usually in clusters; we occupy those fields that have been the most accepting of women: human resources, some communications (senior level positions, but few CEOs), finance, real estate, insurance, and wholesale/retail trade industries. In the mid-1990s, 75 percent of us were employed in these industries. According to the 1995 Commission report, our best opportunities lie in newer industries where the business is fast growing and there isn't a history of any sort of discrimination: for example, in business services; telecommunications, when the industry was viable (because of lots of restructuring and deregulation); and other industries with a female-intensive workforce such as insurance and banking. Perhaps had more women been at the helm of companies such as WorldCom, Global Crossing, Qwest, and Enron, hundreds of thousands of people would still have jobs and pension funds.

It has also been documented, by the original glass ceiling studies and by many organizations, headhunters, writers, and researchers since, that to make it to the top, employees need broad and varied experience in all core areas of a business. This experience comes from access to information, international positions, networking and mentoring, understanding the corporate culture, and, of course, long, hard work. We excel at very long, hard work.

The results from the updated glass ceiling study and the research were not at all surprising. We learned over the years that there still is a very mighty, very sturdy glass ceiling. Those of us who have or have had a management position with very clear possibilities or hopes of getting to the top know all the obvious ramifications of a glass ceiling that have often not permitted us to break through. Carolyn Baldwin Byrd, CEO of GlobalTech Financial, sums up:

> I didn't see discrepancy in promotions or salary until I got to the very top levels, when things other than performance start making a difference. At that level, it is a promotion kind of thing, not a salary differential. Gender never made a difference until you reach the glass ceiling. I think that women in corporate America, in general, have reached glass ceilings, that's why many of them, like myself, are going out and starting their own businesses. We have the credentials; we have the experience, the expertise and the credibility to do that, which is a way around it (the glass ceiling). I don't think you could necessarily consider it discrimination, against women and/or minorities, outright. You get to a point where you are a trailblazer. And that is what we have been since we have been in corporate America. That is what we have been—trailblazers.

The reality is that many very senior male executives are just downright uncomfortable with women in the boardroom, as stereotypical as it may be. Men at the top in their fifties or older are often unable to separate their own insecurities vis à vis women competing with them. They don't know our rules. They can't really psych us out because we are not like them. We aren't them, and, for the most part, we don't aspire to be them either. They don't like the competition against women; it bruises their male egos, and they are scared stiff. Men are uncomfortable with women in close proximity when the relationship is purely professional. They fear the gossip that can arise from too many late meetings, dinners, and

overseas travel. Some fear their own weakness. They don't want to rock
the boat or change a comfort zone.

Dianne Stokely, senior vice president–customer services at FedEx in
Memphis, knows what happens when we instill discomfort in male colleagues, albeit incomprehensible to us: "It is there (the glass ceiling) and
it has affected me. It comes down to the guys being uncomfortable with
us. If I had been a male I do think I would be running this company. It
sounds egotistical, but I really believe it. There is one promotion I surely
did not get because I was female. It sounds horrible but it is true. I
would have had I been 'one of the guys'."

For anyone to resolutely state that the barriers have come down would
be a disservice to all the women, young and old, working themselves to
the bone and finding they're chasing their own tails instead. Everyone
is more aware now than before about what the glass ceiling means, and
what it means not just to women, but to the corporation as a whole. As
we will see in Part II of this book, the issue is much deeper. The glass
ceiling issue questions our standards, our comfort levels, and our competence. If women are the squeaky wheel, they lose by retaliation. If they
are nice, they lose because of niceness. A few women stand out as examples, so when women scream ceiling, some standout and most men
point to the unique women who made it through.

We can count them on one hand, but at least one more is making it
through. And that is what's important. Karen Elliott House, publisher,
the *Wall Street Journal,* observed:

> Every woman who succeeds encourages people to take a chance on
> chance. As they look at it, to take a chance on a woman. As you get
> higher up the pyramid, people have a greater need for camaraderie, for
> confiding and that men still find easier to do with men. If the CEO is
> male, then it would be male. I had a female VP and it is just easier to
> talk to her. I didn't have problems with men, but this was easier.

So, we know the government identified a glass ceiling in 1991. We
know the Federal Glass Ceiling Commission studied and researched the
situation *ad absurdio* and presented its report in 1995. Yet Reuters,[7] at
the start of this millennium, ran a story on a study by two professors at
Simmons College in Boston, Debra Myerson and Joyce K. Fletcher, entitled "Barriers to Women in Workplace Persist." The story excerpted
Myerson and Fletcher's article, "A Modest Manifesto for Shattering the
Glass Ceiling," which appeared in the January 2000 edition of *Harvard
Business Review.*[8] The authors of the *HBR* article contended that "despite

efforts to break the so-called 'glass-ceiling' in the workplace, barriers to women in business persist in subtle ways that can be corrected." And while companies believe they are doing the right thing, the right way, "solutions often amount to essentially teaching women to act like men, or channeling women into jobs for which they are 'well-suited.'" We know that that can be the kiss of death.

Women have much to offer without wasting precious efforts on becoming something we are not. We won't succeed as one of the boys and we'll always feel wanting if we resign ourselves to women-suited careers only.

To be part of the upper echelons in business, we also need to penetrate the boardroom alongside men. This is where the dialogue is taking place. This is the inner sanctum. Our representation on corporate boards remains insufficient. And if we are there, our responsibilities are usually softer than the men's, we are tokens, or we are lumped together by gender and race so it looks better.

Although several of the women I spoke with are on corporate boards, only Sue Kronick, vice chair of Federated Department Stores, underscored the importance of women having a seat on these boards:

> I think the real glass ceiling is in the boardroom. The kind of things you are exposed to through other CEOs in other businesses is an extremely broadening activity. It lifts you out of what you are doing and forces you to look at things in even bigger ways. It accelerates your thinking about diverse principles and how they apply to your business. I think the personal relationships, connections, and interrelated ideas that occur in the boardroom can create unique opportunities. Women clearly are not there. When you think about American industry, that lack of exposure in the boardrooms cuts women out of a very big and important network. They will get there if companies are very proactive about it. It's an important thing for female executives to do.
>
> I joined the board of The Pepsi Bottling Group in March of 1999 with full support from Federated. Some companies don't like their executives spending that kind of time. It has made me a better thinker. The power of the board experience lies with the people you work with. It is a great use of time.

As disturbing as the male/female parallel executive track is, the problem is not just a glass ceiling but a glass ceiling that women perpetuate. Frankly, if we don't band together to shatter it, we will never fully go beyond to the power strata. We know the ceiling exists, because we have bumped our heads against it. But when we walked away, or when we walk away now, we disregard the power we leave on the table, a power we could have if we teamed up and pushed through. If we don't fulfill our part as role models, and we mentor only when it is mandated by the company or seen as favorable to our own getting ahead, we perpetuate a glass ceiling. If, however, we take it upon ourselves to gather a singular energy, we will break through once and for all.

Carol Aynsley, vice president, business development, Medical City Dallas, no longer feels motivated to push through the ceiling by herself. It has been such a long, difficult road that many of us lost that fire in our bellies:

> I think there definitely is a glass ceiling. And when I think of breaking it I realize that it would take everything out of me and I can't stand the game. It normally would be my nature to want to break it. Then I wonder if I am so burned out.
>
> With the glass ceiling, you have to figure out how you are going to play the game inside that company, what are the politics inside that company and are you willing to do what it is going to take to do it? Am I capable, yes; do I want to—no. Want to has more control than capability a lot of times.

We need our colleagues to help form the mass, but more important, we need all the next generations to give it the impetus. What many WEBBs are finding is that these next generations think what we have came naturally. Carolyn Baldwin Byrd of GlobalTech Financial noted:

> A lot of those women in high-level corporate positions right now did not necessarily grow up in the age where they had to go through the struggles. They have sort of ridden the crest. We laid the groundwork for them, we sweated through and have battle scars to show for it too.
>
> The group immediately behind us truly don't understand. They really think they got there on their own. They don't understand the scars, the battles we had to fight and the abuse. The stares and the looks we suffered to lay the groundwork for them.

Without the support of the women following us, we ensure that the glass remains barely dimpled. We have to realize that all the official mandates and all the EEOC and corporate regulations will not easily open doors to the vault for us. We have seen this with other minorities that are legislated into jobs or schools. We know the value and many pitfalls of affirmative action. But we have to help ourselves get through this. The only way to do it is to work with all the younger generations of women who enter the workforce. And to work very closely with them. If we really watched our male counterparts and followed their example, it would be easy. The men who didn't hire us did hire guys who they thought would grow up to be them. They hired surrogate sons. They looked to form these young men in their own image. That is why women never can enter the ranks in that manner. It doesn't mean we have to be like men. We saw that in the 1980s.

Women today have to be mindful of WEBB history. Not doing so may turn the clock back fifty years. We need to understand what came before so we won't be condemned to repeating what went wrong.

Moving up the ranks in business is our boot camp. How we survive boot camp depends on how we face a myriad of obstacles. As Nietzsche said, "Obstacles are those frightful things you see when you take your eyes off your goals."

NOTES

1. We discuss the choices we made or that were made for us in more detail in Part II, chapter 10.

2. Susan Faludi, *Backlash: The Undeclared War against American Women* (New York: Crown, 1991), p. 368.

3. Executive Summary Fact Finding Report of the Federal Glass Ceiling Commission, Section 1, Introduction, Overview and Highlights of Research, 1995, p. 3.

4. U.S. Bureau of Labor Statistics, "Highlights of Women's Earnings in 2001," Report 960, May 2002.

5. Aaron Donovan, "No Gains for Women on Corporate Boards," *New York Times*, June 24, 2001.

6. Op. cit., p. 6.

7. Reuters, "Barriers to Women in Workplace Persist," January 7, 2000.

8. "A Modest Manifesto for Shattering the Glass Ceiling," *Harvard Business Review,* January 1, 2000.

Part II

THE TWENTY-FIRST CENTURY

Chapter 2

DIVIDED WE FALL

As they say on Wall Street, "Don't fight the trend, the trend is your friend."

What they say is: You've got to be part of the solution or else you are part of the problem.

What they mean is: You are a problem and this is a warning.

"'I've said it before and I'll say it again that a woman may very well become a member of Augusta,' Mr. Johnson, known as Hootie, said in an interview. 'But that is sometime off in the future, which wouldn't suggest that it's on the horizon. In the meantime, we hold dear our tradition and constitutional right to choose.' "[1]

We expected more. By this time, in this century, we deserved more. We thought we left that old generation behind in the twentieth century. Clearly, the roots are deep, and what was created fifty years ago often finds its offspring making the rules today.

If we had to identify the root of the difficulties women face in the workplace, it is the old rule of military law and ranks. Woman cannot assume that just because we are smart or work harder, we will get the promotion that eventually leads to CEO. Deep-rooted rank-and-rule laws have been passed down through generations of men. They are as applicable to aging grandfathers as to their grandsons who are now running corporate America. Following these unspoken laws maintains their comfort zone. The same principles hold true for sports. It is their team. Don't mess with the system.

Sports and the military—women are making strides in both. Forty percent of the athletes in the 2000 Olympics in Sydney were women, and they participated in 44 percent of the total number of events, according to the official Olympic organization Web site. In 2002, women made up 37 percent of the participants. And the women's bobsled event was brought back. We have made fine strides over the last several centuries. Consider, for example, that married women were barred from the ancient Olympic Games (although prostitutes or virgins were allowed to watch). The purse was not all that great for early women athletes, either. Pomegranates, symbols of fertility, were prizes at the women's games, along with olive wreaths and a slice of a sacrificial cow. Men, however, got women as prizes in ancient Olympic chariot races. Our purses are still slim compared with men's, but they are more than a pomegranate. And they don't get us as prizes anymore.

Nor are we accepted in all sports venues. We may be allowed to play at Augusta some time in the future. But not now. The exclusionary policy is an embarrassment to many of the elite members of this hallowed golf course. But the fact that we have to make such a stink about membership is an even greater embarrassment to the women who want in and to the women who would like it not to be an issue.

A deep-rooted bias follows men into the workplace, which is an inability to bypass authority or a chain of command. It is the same for the military and for sports. Although part of the game, women are not trained the same; it is almost impossible for us to accept certain things at face value. Many male executives tend, as they did with their Little League coaches, to accept authority on blind faith; they show the expected measure of respect and question little or nothing. They learn at an early age not to blatantly question authority or to demonstrate raw individuality until the timing is right. Asking is one thing, questioning is another. They follow the rules. They are insiders. They don't have to prove they are better than the team. They don't want to, either. Maybe one guy is considered the star athlete but guys won't even question that. Women do. Nothing is worse than another woman, for all appearances equal, who is considered better, prettier, smarter, richer, or more important. If we could ever rid ourselves of that instinctive envy, we would make astonishing strides. If we could learn to stop discriminating against ourselves, men might not feel all that empowered to discriminate against us. Even in sports, women can't seem to get interest from their own or for their own. For example, much hullabaloo accompanied the advent of women's basketball, yet within a few years several of the teams have folded. The fan base for the women's teams grew too slowly to keep these franchises going, and corporations, dying to get center stage for the Knicks or Bulls, have no interest in giving equal support to women's teams. It is the same for tennis, soccer, or slalom.

Not being seen as a team player, however, is a surefire reason why many women are not promoted. And why there are not more of us at the helm. Being hired does not automatically put a woman or man, for that matter, on track. A friend of mine was telling me about her son, a salesman at one of the top Wall Street firms. During a period of severe layoffs, he managed to survive. And although he suffered some sleepless nights, because he was considered a team player, the firm found a place for him after disbanding the rest of his department. He would not have received the same good fortune if he had been a loner or perceived to be aloof. It is all about comfort. Comfort of the folks who are bringing you along. And later on, comfort of those you are bringing along.

If you doubt the power of the sports analogy, you are mightily out of touch with the present working world. You just need to go into a CEO's office or check out the power booths at football and baseball fields. The offices are decorated with important team memorabilia. Major corporations, banks, and agencies sponsor all the boxes and sports suites. Seats to important games are coveted, and usually it is the top guys who get the invitations.

A team has an anima of its own. When they lose, the coach gives a long, rousing pep talk; the players know in their hearts that they will win the next time. That never happens with girls—not as girls, not as women. If we lose once, we have to have the self-confidence to brush off the hurt and humiliation, hold back the tears welling in our eyes, and go on. No one is out there cheering for us.

To really succeed in this millennium, women will have to get full support from their constituents: peers, superiors, and employees. We can't just be better and brighter and have more integrity. There is power in numbers, and women have to understand that. But as Margaret Mead is quoted as saying: "Girls don't learn to cooperate with anybody."

The inability to "behave" as expected is one reason why so many talented women forgo the corporate experience to become successful entrepreneurs. Sometimes it seems easier to just do it alone than to try and buck this kind of system.

For those who want to move up within the system, however, the task becomes arduous. How do we break through? We get so far but not there, not to the top. The play is subtler now. There is no open combat, and men expect to see us around in all but the very highest levels, sometimes even in the boardroom. As with any racial issue, lots of men just don't see a gender difference. They don't separate women but rather just expect to see a diverse group of men and women, whites, African Americans, Hispanics. That is, diversity is accepted as natural, even more so in large cities. But for all of these men, there are too many still stuck and uncomfortable. They can't get beyond the male-female interaction.

Dianne Stokely, senior vice president–customer services at FedEx, finds that women are left unhinged by the team player issue. "They always say 'she' is not a team player. But when it has happened against me I have been lucky to have someone stick up for me. That can be a fatal accusation." If you were privy to the boardroom at Azurix (an Enron company), where Rebecca Mark had a fate similar to Jill Barad's at Mattel, you might have witnessed that fatal scenario.

Many of the new advice books for women tell us not to do the work to make the boss look good. We should be selfish and self-serving. But in the long run, that negative behavior works against us. It makes us appear nonmanagerial, not team players, and/or detrimental to the good vibes and success of the company. Even worse, management comes to see us a part of the problem and not part of the solution. Then we are damned to never breaking through the vice president level.

The women I interviewed for this book succeeded in the corporate world and moved up the ranks by not becoming problems. Not one was a troublemaker or an activist. Not one bucked the trend or fought to remove a mediocre male superior. The women succeeded by ensuring that they were part of the solution. Each one of them surely had at least one mediocre supervisor in her career and more important, a supporter, maybe even a mentor. The others either spoke out (troublemaker) or left because a situation became intolerable.

The paucity of mentors for women as they move up the career track has not changed over the last few decades. As several studies have noted, strong mentorship is critical to how women will succeed in future decades because it affects a majority of good, sound businesswomen who may not rise to CEO but who will surely become fine senior executives.

There are probably many reasons that women don't consider mentoring or role modeling important to their own futures. Some are so stereotyped they are embarrassing. For example, women in all age groups tend to dismiss another woman because of her looks, her marital status, her education, or her talents. And if she is famous, it is far worse. She had better find some tragedy in her life that all the other women can relate to. In the long run this does not bode well for us. This emotion surfaces early on in life. Unless mothers teach their daughters to play fair with their playmates and forgive their shortcomings, their pretty dresses, their doll collection, or, worse, their virtues, they will have only a slight chance of overcoming these feelings by the time they start their careers. And they have to forgive the next generation of younger, maybe better educated or better prepared women and, instead of competing, become allies and mentors.

For years we blamed the men. It was their fault that we didn't succeed. We never even thought that we could be just as guilty. So, decades ago, we believed that once fair employment and antidiscrimination laws were passed by Congress, we'd be home free. We cheered the creation of the Equal Employment Opportunity Commission (EEOC), even though it meant very little when the first wave of female baby boomers started pounding the pavement for work.

The creation in 1965 of the EEOC by the U.S. government was intended to stop the discrimination that was so rampant in business. The commission has come into its own over the decades. And although the EEOC may not encourage women to accuse their company of discrimination or other unlawful acts, it will support despicable cases. Yet, discrimination is still very tough to prove.

Discrimination: the mere mention of the word is enough to send shudders up and down the spine. We hoped the word would be extinct by now. Yet not a week or two goes by without some article appearing in the newspaper documenting a study on position, power, pay, overall parity. Where we are is not where we hoped to be in this century.

How do you prove discrimination when it can be so subtle? Do you stamp your foot and ask why you didn't get the sales leads? Or the promotion? Protesting too much might call attention to you as a troublemaker and could give management a reason to push you out. They close rank around you, surrounding you like a herd of elephants, and unless you are very confident, very convinced, and probably very foolish, you get squashed. Hostility you could cut with a knife emerges. If you are really unlucky, it can follow you around in the industry. As with the scarlet letter, only women get the honor. A man with a drug problem, a philanderer, a cheat, or a liar may get a slap on the wrist or may leave one company and get a better, higher-paid job at the competition. Women don't. They are branded.

You only need to review Alison Schieffelin's complaint, victory, and ultimate sacking at Morgan Stanley.

In June 2000, Morgan Stanley, the prestigious Wall Street investment firm, was cited for discrimination against women. Turns out that they had discriminated against Alison Schieffelin who had brought the suit against the company. The fact is that to get that far with the EEOC, she was, in all probability, the only woman who had the courage to endure the consequences and eventual retaliation against her by coworkers (male and female) and management. Ms. Schieffelin complained that less-deserving men had been promoted to the position of managing director. The EEOC, according to the *New York Times*, said it had "seen evidence of 'a pattern and practice' of discrimination against women employed in Morgan Stanley's institutional stocks division."[2] The verdict was a major victory for all women on Wall Street and very long in coming. Practically every woman who works or worked in a Wall Street firm has experienced painful, possibly even humiliating, discrimination at some time in her career. Complaints to management or even the company EEO office have been ignored and lawsuits have been thrown out, dismissed, overturned, or just left on the table; many women either burn out or give up the fight for fear of the consequences.

Four months after the verdict, Schieffelin was fired. Morgan Stanley alleged that the cause was a "result of disruptive and insubordinate behavior toward her direct supervisor," according to the *New York Times* follow-up article.[3] The commission did not find that credible and allowed that Morgan Stanley had "reduced information and resources which it had previously provided to Ms. Schieffelin." Withholding information and resources is one way to make someone's life a living hell in the investment business.

Ms. Schieffelin's situation underscores an indispensable survival secret for boot camp. The men and women who succeed in the kind of environment found at Morgan Stanley, or any similar firm, don't buck the system. Schieffelin assessed her situation and, win or lose, went for it all the way. She was extremely brave, and one would expect that she knew the probable consequences. Her environment at work following the original verdict could not have been a day at the park.

As a footnote to the Schieffelin case, the EEOC did in fact sue Morgan Stanley. While investigating the treatment of women in the firm's investment banking division since Schieffelin's complaint, it had contacted other women and amassed files of information on Morgan Stanley's hiring practices. It should be noted that Ms. Schieffelin, earning $1 million a year, was no slouch.[4]

In the early days, women were made to believe that we—not by sex but by intellect—were if not inferior, at least not knowledgeable about the business we were in on Wall Street. This condemnation was perfected during the 1980s backlash when WEBBs were moving into the workplace in meaningful numbers. But in those days, when we knew we knew what we knew, we were still unable to touch the holy grail of high level positions. The partnerships, the directorships, the executive floor—all were beyond our reach. Those who were more compliant and more accepting were helped along precisely because they would never upset the status quo and were of no threat. That was about the same time when our bosses started talking about us being part of the solution and not the problem. It was a catchall that could be used against us. And often was. The last thing you wanted to be called was a troublemaker. Ultimately, that was Alison Schieffelin's downfall.

The distressing thing is that this silent sparring must result in litigation for us to be taken seriously. Not one of us had that in mind. "The women following us now will have an opportunity to go a lot higher than we did as a result of the lawsuits. They will be able to get to the next level of management that we failed to reach. I see that happening now. Any company right now that doesn't have its act in order deserves to get what it gets. These lawsuits are a sign of the times," adds Carolyn Baldwin Byrd, CEO of GlobalTech Financial and former assistant treasurer of the Coca-Cola Company.

American Express recently settled a class action suit brought by four women, followed by thirteen more, who filed a complaint with the EEOC claiming they were discriminated against in pay and denied promotions. It is the same glass ceiling contention. According to an Associated Press report on June 18, 2002, "The women said the financial services giant created a 'glass ceiling' for female financial advisors by giving lucrative accounts and steering leads on prospective clients to male advisors, and by favoring men in training, mentoring and promotion."[5] The company paid a cash settlement and agreed to begin mandatory diversity training, and ensure that 32 percent of new hires are women.

Barely a month goes by without an article in the *New York Times* detailing bias, disparities, or discrimination against women. In June 2002, the "National Women's Law Center, a nonprofit group representing women on economic, education and workplace issues, analyzed enrollment figures in high school vocational and technical courses nationwide."[6] Not surprisingly, women were directed into becoming cosmeticians and health aides, while men were steered toward becoming electricians and plumbers, earning sometimes twice what the women made.

In May 2002, the *Times* reported "racial and sexual disparities in employment at the nation's weapons laboratories."[7] Disparities were found at the three national weapons labs run by the Energy Department. The investigation by the General Accounting Office, requested by two congressional representatives, found that salaries for minority men and women, and for white women, were generally lower than for white males. White males were also found to hold a greater percentage of managerial and professional jobs, 64 percent, than their representation in the workforce, about 54 percent.

In July 2002, an article in the *New York Times* stated that results of a study by two Rutgers Law professors found that "Women and minorities appear to be benefiting from greater employment opportunities in the United States, but discrimination remains a significant problem."[8]

And this discrimination is not just in business. In another July 2002 article, the *Times* reported that women seeking tenure at several top universities are being denied the lifetime security because of "collegiality." Teamwork. Female academics are not seen as part of the group. "Male professors, too, have complained about being penalized for perceived disagreeable personality traits. But some academics say collegiality evaluations can be a particular obstacle for women who are self-promoting, hard-edged or otherwise outside female social norms." One female professor denied tenure was described by a male colleague as "stellar." The colleague added that "his experience elsewhere had been that women who came up for tenure in the sciences were often criticized as being pushy and aggressive."[9]

Many men will immediately counter that we are doing too much whining. Whining is too reactive, and while we must know what we are facing, we have gotten too far to let it ruin our day. All these reports indicate that the mandates, the diversity programs, the mentoring programs don't guarantee our pathway to the executive suite. And since no one is going to carry us forward on his shoulders, it ultimately rests on our own to make this happen for us and for the women coming up after us. The secret to this is making those teams work and understanding that we need each other to succeed. As the author Charles Brower said, "Few people are successful unless a lot of other people want them to be."

We have to be the other people. And we have to support the success of other women. We can't keep looking at successful women with envy and bad-mouthing them because of their achievements. "Women are catty and jealous of other women. If you have more than I do then I'll be upset until I have more than you. More of it and better, that is the way they feel," notes Carolyn Baldwin Byrd.

Women often are portrayed as evil. We get to be the mean witch, the evil stepmother, the villainess. There are no fairy tales about evil stepfathers.

A colleague of mine had a terrible time at her company. According to another colleague: "She was undone by her people because she was perceived to be the bitch. But it wouldn't have happened if she were a man. One of the guys she hired filed a complaint that she discriminated against him because of his ethnic background. There was some bad stuff about her departure." This woman was very good at what she did. She had darts thrown at her from both sides. Her employees resented her and her boss (male) feared for his own career because she was so much stronger than he. She didn't get support from other women either. So she had to go. Her company had mandates and support in place, but they did not protect her.

Linda Wachner, former chairman and CEO of Warnaco Group made her reputation as a smart, brassy, ruthless businesswoman and became one of the highest paid and most successful female CEOs in the United States. Wachner rode to the top but teed off so many people on the way that when problems in the company could no longer be concealed, she found she was defending herself alone as employees, colleagues, clients, and associates were cheering her ultimate demise.

Women have been attacked about everything but the quality of our work, if we are lucky. If not, we are attacked about the work as well. Consider Bryant Gumbel. The man whined his way through years of early morning and failed prime-time television. Whether or not he is a personal choice among commentators is of little interest. But what he said about his former female cohosts does have some relevance. The *Miami Herald* ran a vignette about Gumbel and comments he made regarding Katie Couric. He griped that he was unappreciated vis-à-vis Katie, and that he deserved as many accolades as she did for the success of the show during their time together. Then he went and got mean. She wasn't as perky as viewers thought and she "went through five assistants in five years, three or four makeup and hair people and had a prime-time news show that failed to make the grade."[10] That attack was below the belt. Too many women have been undone by similar spitefulness from male associates. Men have bitched and gotten away with it, not all that often in the mass media, but surely in the boardroom where they can speak in confidentiality with their mostly male allies. Even if we knew about the mean-spirited gossip face-to-face, it is awfully hard to fight those allegations without shouting libel. And rarely is that a viable option, not if we want to keep on working. Besides which, we may never even know about it except when we are denied a promotion. We are too easy a mark for this kind of verbal attack.

Perhaps Katie did have five assistants in so many years. Why does this become greater than it is? Perhaps she is demanding, perhaps the assistants expected something or someone else. If this had been a man with five assistants over that period of time, would we even know about it? Would the comment even have been made? Would it have bitch written all over it?

Through the years I have seen many men treat their staff—men and women—worse than poorly. But it never became an issue. Both sexes took it as a payment of dues. Unless it was excessively abusive. Or more recently, unless there was a hint of harassment. Often, it was the way these men worked. We WEBBs hated it. We may have cried, but we took it. Such men were the coaches screaming abusively at their team even though their reactions might often have been exaggerated. But no one would ever make the derogatory remarks about a male boss that are made about a female boss. "She's too emotional." "She doesn't know how to relax." "She's just a bitch." "Probably has more balls than her husband." "No wonder she can't find a husband . . . lover . . . companion . . . " "Her kids can't even stand her." "Her secretary says . . . " ad infinitum.

I was surprised one day by a male friend of mine during a conversation about a female U.S. senator. The first time I just ignored the comment that she was a bitch. Then in a later conversation about a woman CEO, the same friend and another very close friend called her a bitch as well. Now I know both these men very well. They are both unbiased regarding women in the workplace. Both have hired and supported women and have wives, and one a daughter, who are professionals. Yet it was understood that these women, to get into their positions of power, had to be bitches. When I brought this up in conversation, both looked at me in total surprise. Well, yes they agreed that these particular women were probably bitches, but not all women in power were that way. I brought up the Katie Couric situation because it had surfaced in another context, not including Bryant Gumbel's senseless and unnecessary comments. And, yup, according to them, she was probably a bitch, too. There are probably many bitches out there. It is a plague. But as a man loses his temper, acts irrationally, makes excessive demands, he will just always be seen as the ultimate company guy, a go-getter. She will always be the bitch.

Male colleagues often ask me, how come women are like that? Meaning their own worst professional enemies. I think that women often get crummy advice. We are advised to be more aggressive than the next woman, step on any other woman's toes, go for it, and take no prisoners. And men, as we know, are brought up in teams—baseball, basketball, and football. "Guys don't have these issues, they have teams. Women just generally feel that they have to be better. Some of the younger women are thinking that, but they are not sure it is real or coming from the inside," says Sharon Brown, assistant dean, administration and development, University of Miami School of Business and former partner at Coopers & Lybrand. They were old boy networkers in college fraternities. The mind-set was not to destroy and conquer but to rally the troops and then conquer. Boys were brought up to respect their teammates. They didn't fight against the team, it wouldn't be sportsmanlike and they risked getting kicked off by the coach. Remember, the coach is Boss; his orders are gospel.

As the highest-ranking woman officer at a major international rating agency remarked: "Now I am out of the trenches, on top of the bunker. But when I was in the trenches, women were absolutely more intimidated by other women being more successful and had more trouble working with other women than with male counterparts."

The secret of teamwork is not found in the creation of a team. It is much larger than that. Although researchers can gauge how far women have come in terms of salary and salary discrepancies,[11] they can't measure levels of support or the inevitable gossiping about women as they move up the ladder.

You won't succeed on your own. You can ask the walking wounded. John Dunne told us centuries ago that "No man is an island." That holds true for women, too. Sue Kronick, vice chair of Federated Department Stores, Inc. believes:

> Most people focus on tactics. You need to worry less about coming up with a solution than about finding the right people to help get you there. You build alignment, consensus, involvement. People are part of solving the problem. I think that many women do build consensus and collaboration better than men. You are at your most confident when you are willing not to know, when you are willing to reach out to other people, when you are open."

The secret is to rally the troops. Then we conquer.

NOTES

1. Clifton Brown, "At Club in Augusta, Policy of Chairman Remains 'Men Only,'" *New York Times,* November 12, 2002.

2. Patrick McGeehan, "Morgan Stanley Is Cited for Discrimination Against Women," *New York Times,* June 6, 2000.

3. Patrick McGeehan, "Morgan Stanley May Face Sex-Discrimination Suit," *New York Times,* September 7, 2001.

4. The lawsuit continues and a trial may forever be elusive. After several years, both sides, the EEOC, and Morgan Stanley were unable to settle the lawsuit. The commission that took up Alison Schieffelin's case and sued Morgan Stanley implied that they may be representing more than 100 women in the full case, according to a follow-up in *The New York Times* by Patrick McGeehan, the reporter covering the story. The article, "Morgan Stanley and U.S. Agency Fail to Settle Sex Bias Lawsuit," appeared in the *Times* on April 16, 2003.

5. Associated Press, "American Express Settles Bias Lawsuit," June 18, 2002. Published in *Miami Herald.*

6. Diane Jean Schemo, "Group Says Course Training Still Breaks Along Sex Lines," *New York Times,* June 7, 2002.

7. Warren E. Leary, "Report Finds Disparities in Hiring at U.S. Labs," *New York Times,* May 22, 2002.

8. Reed Abelson, "Study Finds Bias on the Job Still Common," *New York Times,* July 24, 2002.

9. Tamar Lewin, "'Collegiality' as a Tenure Battleground," *New York Times,* July 12, 2002.

10. Howard Cohen, "Professional Whiner," *Miami Herald,* October 25, 1999.

11. More on that in chapter 11.

Chapter 3

NUMEROLOGY AND A
HANDHELD COMPUTER

If the world was perfect, it wouldn't be.

—Yogi Berra

The most obvious shift starting with the WEBB generation was into technology. In technology, you could be female or male, pretty or not, it didn't matter. In the end, technology seemed to be a perfect equalizer. Women entering tech fields in the early days were "unanimous in their belief that the micro industry welcomes women much more warmly than many other industries," remarked Ann Winblad, a prominent Silicon Valley venture capitalist. This "industry is unique. It's one of the few industries created out of thin air. You're judged totally on competence, you can't bluff your way. That puts women on an equal basis. Here you can be a smart mutt with no pedigree and jump right in."[1]

In high school, WEBBs could take one of two roads—math/science or verbal/literature/languages. I never really thought about math again until after I had already started my MBA. Even then, the distinction of having excelled in math was not a fully conscious bit of enlightenment. But it is so clear now. Of all the women I interviewed for this book, the college math majors were the ones who had the least difficult time maneuvering their way into the business world. It makes so much sense, but early on those who pursued a career with math either became teachers or skilled office workers. No one really expected to parlay the degree into a high management position. Not at the outset. It soon became evident that there were opportunities to be seized, but you had to be there to know that.

I did some totally unscientific research to back up my claim that a facility for numbers made a tremendous difference for WEBBs entering business. I always used VURs, or very unscientific research studies, to gauge trends and behavior patterns, and I would bet the house on them. Peter Lynch used something similar in picking stocks. He spoke to people to find out what they were thinking and who was buying what, using what, watching what, and doing what. It worked. He was one of the most successful portfolio managers of all time. Well, this is similar. I asked lots of questions of lots of women. I found that those women who were most successful didn't just have an aptitude for math and science, but majored in it, often got a graduate degree in it. They were taken the most seriously at the entry level, and they were the ones who seemed to move up with the least effort.

Janet, president at one of the top international public relations agencies in Florida, loved writing, which ultimately underscored her success in public relations, but it was math that got her into business as a start: "Actually, I wanted to be a math teacher. I loved it. I got into advanced calculus in college."

Jean Thresher, MD, also thought math teaching would be fun but never felt compelled to follow the pattern set for the WEBBs as teachers or nurses. Her mother, once a child prodigy with a genius IQ, was an extraordinary woman and a composer of classical music. Now in her eighties, her mother is still an activist of renown for environmental issues in the Florida Keys. Jean noted:

> First, I wanted to be a math teacher. I wanted something I could do while the children were small and that I could go back to. My mother didn't push that on me. She always worked and was not home very much. When I finished my math degree, I decided to go into computer programming because that fit those same requirements. I could do it initially, could stop for a while, and then could do at home while the children were small.

Decades later, Jean is a gynecologist practicing in Ohio. I had never even heard of computers in those days.

Ellen Hancock experienced much the same. She majored in math and logic. Right from the start, she had ambition and talent. The one company to recognize her gift in those days, the 1960s, was IBM, and they hired her on as a junior programmer after she received her master's degree in math. The rest of her story is history.

I first saw Ellen Hancock at IBM, when she was head of their Networking division. Ellen was the first woman to reach senior management at Big Blue. But when Lou Gerstner joined the company and created his core management team, Ellen was not included and found herself out of a job and the company after almost three decades. Eventually, she rejoined her former mentor, Gil Amelio, at Apple Computer for his ill-fated stint there. Once again she got axed when Steve Jobs returned to the company and pushed Amelio out. She didn't fade away but rather ended up as president and chief executive officer of Exodus Communications, a company that ran the back-office computer centers that powered Web sites like Yahoo and eBay. The technology meltdown that began in March 2000 was not kind to the Internet sector or to any company whose business derived from it. Exodus was no exception, and the company tumbled out of favor and finally into bankruptcy. Ellen Hancock resigned before the filing. For a time, Hancock's worth in stock was greater than both her nemeses.

But what can you do if you didn't major in mathematics or computer sciences or economics? Success in the business world is not ephemeral. Women aren't running major brokerage houses or investment banks—yet. But they are gaining ground in many of the top financial institutions. Many of these women were liberal arts majors, who had smarts, ambition, and career goals. They just didn't know what those goals were, or at least, which roads would get them to the bigger goals of success that they had in mind. They were open to new fields and to learning from the bottom up. That was so with the WEBB generation and is true now. Except that now, too many young women want to skip the initial steps, paying the dues, so to speak. Diane de Vries Ashley, a director, the Private Bank for Bank of America, told me the following:

> I hadn't a clue what I wanted to be when I was young. I wound up in banking for a very simple reason—my husband to be at that point had a friend at Banker's Trust; he introduced me and I walked out with a job. I had no clue that I was ever going to go into banking. I didn't even know what it was. I was not particularly good in math. You can always hire people to do the mathematical parts, you need the personal side. On the other hand, they didn't hire me for their training program. I was hired as a secretary and administration assistant. I was not expected to progress beyond that. You were actively discouraged to show ambition. What saved me was that one of the people around me discovered that I spoke five languages. He thought he could use those skills. He was very instrumental in helping me develop. It became clear to me that if I wanted to go anywhere I'd need to go through the training program, which after some

pushing on my side, they allowed me into three years later. My inspiration
to go into banking was dumb luck and it turned out that I was good at it.

Dianne Stokely, senior vice president–customer services of FedEx,
ended up in business because she was convinced she could make more
money and pay for a hairdresser, instead of becoming one:

I first became a bookkeeper but knew that accounting was the way I
wanted to go, I really liked it. I realized that as a woman if you specialized,
that gave you a heads-up. As a generalist, you could easily be cast aside.
But as a specialist, you had something you could ride. I came to work at
FedEx in the early days; the company was only one year old. They were
looking for employees constantly; they weren't making any money in
those days. I went and interviewed with a woman, and the interviewer
was the sister-in-law of someone I had worked for several years before.
So she made me a job offer right there. I took it because I had two kids
and $50 in my pocket. I was a full-charge bookkeeper, but I had to take
a job as accounts payable clerk. Through a stroke of luck I became an
associate accountant, which was actually a bookkeeper. The woman who
had the job had to take a leave and they gave me the job on a temporary
basis—but I did such a good job that when the woman came back they
gave her my job. I got a $200-a-month raise. I had never gotten more than
a $50-a-month raise. So I decided I would never leave FedEx. But I still
didn't have my degree and it was suggested that I finish it.

I became a financial analyst after I got my degree and worked in the
finance area for ten years. During this time, too, I got my MBA—working
full time, going to school at night. My last financial position was when I
was promoted into a job as chief financial person for one of our operating
regions. Then after eighteen months I was promoted to a director of field
operations. I was the first finance person to be promoted into this high
level of operations. And then I was promoted to a larger district doing the
same thing. I have had to prove myself over and over again. Every time
something else comes up, someone says I'm not sure she can do it. And
I do do it.

The aptitude for math and science is important. But more important
for success is being a sponge for new information. That's an attribute all
these women share, even today, even as they have proven themselves
and hold key executive positions. Mary Barneby majored in philosophy
and psychology. She had no training or guidance and, nevertheless, ended
up on Wall Street.

I just kind of found myself there because I needed a job. When I was
there I began to learn and experience and continue my education from a

business perspective. I realize that I hadn't taken any undergraduate courses to prepare me. But it just seemed like it was the way to grow both intellectually, financially, and personally. Resourcefulness really drove me there and allowed me to enjoy the challenges of learning something new.

I went to work for Merrill Lynch from college—I wanted to get a graduate degree but took a temporary job at Merrill because I was a bit burned out from academia. When I interviewed there they were under a consent decree from government to hire women and minorities over the next few years. When I graduated, I went to Europe for six months, and when I came back I took job as a secretary for a university development office in New York. I was there for a few months, but it was terribly boring. Then I saw an ad that Merrill was looking for women to hire as account executives. I took the financial aptitude test. They said I did fine and asked if I wanted to go into a broker-training program. But I really didn't then. It was an idealistic time, and I felt that going there was going to work for the enemy by selling securities. They gave me a job anyway, in their systems department, going around the company doing efficiency studies to see where they should automate and where they should move from manual procedures to data processing. That really got me interested. I worked throughout the whole company. I liked working, I liked learning, producing results. There was so much to learn. I didn't have this feeling that I had to be an assistant vice president, or the sense of entitlement. I was like a sponge and learned so much. Very few people, or women, if any, went on to business school from college. Most who did went years later, as I did. There was a sense of "just do it" and just figure it out. If you want to be there, then be there and work hard.

Mary's concern though, is that we are losing the resourcefulness that allowed women like us to muddle through without being handed anything or without a sense of entitlement. We were able to go into a situation and learn so much. Figuring it out ourselves makes us more successful, she feels.

Spencer Humphrey, vice president, director of mass market publishing at Scholastic Inc., wanted to work with children but didn't want to waste her time getting a specialized degree in education either in college or afterward. So, like so many liberal arts graduates, she ended up in business by default.

I ended up working for a stockbroking firm in New York. The reason was that A, they hired me, and B, it seemed like an innocuous way to earn money without being someone's secretary. I was an assistant stock trader, an assistant in the trust division in Morgan Guarantee, and I ended up as an institutional salesperson at two different brokerages. That is how I spent my twenties. I was the only woman for miles. There were no women on the Wall Street side of Morgan or on the trading desk. It was fun, a rough-and-tumble game. I had no ambitions in this area; I liked the money, and I liked the freedom and the autonomy. So I worked on Wall Street and played in the theater. But when I got to my late twenties, I realized the business did not have enough meaning for me. I took a course designed for women looking to change careers.

But my first job was on the Street where I had worked as a receptionist the summer before. Then when I graduated they hired me as a trading assistant. I learned the language and the pace of the business. Many of the lessons I learned there have stood me in very good stead throughout my career—not only a richer understanding of business, but how business is done, in terms of the daily operations of business—and I also learned perspective. There was so much money changing hands so quickly in those jobs. You cease to worry so much about making decisions, you become very inured to the decision-making process.

Everything changed for me the day that I looked over that trading desk and had the realization that all of these guys were not smarter than I was, they had no better schooling than I did, and they didn't know anything more than I did about what they were doing. All they had was the courage of their convictions. And I suddenly got it.

I remember the day it happened. I literally looked up over the desk and saw these guys, my colleagues, and it struck me like a bolt of lightning. I had never questioned it—I just knew it. It was just a way of going. I had never questioned it, it was an unconscious question of status. The day that curtain lifted was very very profound.

I thought that all guys were born knowing where the manifold was on the car and understanding what a PE (price earnings) ratio was. That was somehow knowledge that was not for me. Then I got it—they didn't know it, either. They were better at having balls out. I knew that I probably had more balls than they did, I just never had the experience of using them!

I started really selling then, instead of reacting. It started to come together. When I realized I could do it, then I realized it really wasn't what I should be doing. It is only a question of competence, it's not a question of knowledge. It is a question of the competence you bring to any decision-making process.

Before becoming assistant dean at the University of Miami Business School, Sharon Brown was a partner at Coopers & Lybrand. At a young age, Sharon discovered that she had an aptitude for figures. She was brought up believing that you needed to have a skill so that you could always take care of yourself no matter what happened to you in life. In early WEBB days, that meant taking typing in addition to a core curriculum. But she was smart enough to get a scholarship for school so she was able to continue her studies in chemistry, physics, and trigonometry, and she entered college as a math major.

> In the back of my mind, though, I really liked the accounting. All those math and accounting majors had an easier time because they had a skill. Now it is the economy that has changed things. Our students in computer science still have an edge because there is such a need, but it is not perceived the same. I think, though, that some of the softer skills, like being articulate, being creative, are more important than the analytical now. The women I observed in finance and accounting may not have ended up in the discipline years later, but it was the initial skill that got them where they were. It does allow you to reach parity when you come into the workplace and you can branch out from there. It surely helped me.

Anna Rentz, president, Northern Trust Bank, South Florida, went back for her MBA years after graduating from college, years that were spent playing bridge, playing tennis, and making Christmas ornaments. Armed with the degree, Anna, like so many of us with no strong business skills, had no idea what to do next. She went to Southeast Bank (now Bank of America) at the suggestion of one of her friends in Junior League whose husband helped her get into a training program. It was her only interview and is how she got into banking.

> I was afraid they were going to find out that they had made a terrible mistake, that I couldn't do anything, that I didn't know anything, and send me away. But as weeks went by I began to realize that my strong work ethic, my fervent desire to be successful, and my life experiences and connections, given my late start in the business world, just might be enough to propel me along. And it was.

Several years later she got a call from a headhunter about Northern Trust Bank.

> I had never heard of this bank back in 1983, as they were just entering the Florida market. After many interviews and much soul searching, I decided to accept the challenge. I was provided a desk (empty) and a telephone (silent), and I set about trying to build a client base for Northern Trust. Looking back, I feel that I was quite brave to take a chance on my ability to be entrepreneurial. It turned out to be the best move that I ever made. Today, the Florida bank is one of the most profitable banks in the country over $1 billion.

The highest-ranking woman officer at a major international rating agency also had no idea about what to expect or even what was expected of her when she was first hired by the agency. She had considered joining the foreign service or pursuing a career in anthropology. That was after contemplating playing electric guitar in a rock band. But once in graduate school she realized that business, particularly business for government, offered better career opportunities. Armed with her MPA (Master's in Public Administration), she worked in city government before interviewing at the rating agency for an entry-level analyst position. Like the others, she "had no clue," but because more women were being hired in public finance than corporate finance, she joined the ratings side in public finance.

> I came in as an analyst. A few years later I began to move into management. I had supervisors who would tell me what to wear; they were uncomfortable with women or women's issues. But it wasn't as bad as it was in traditional Wall Street firms. There are some really ugly stories out there.

But her experience was relatively positive. "What counted most was your analytical talent and your ability to deal with bankers and issuers."

Like many of the WEBB generation, Karen, former chief financial officer of FedEx Latin America, also wanted to do something to save the world, but she never thought it was going to be through financing anything. Even at college, she "switched majors every week." After graduation she took some accounting courses and discovered it was something she could do. "Being an accountant would give me an element of freedom in terms of the versatility that I could use it for. I thought I could do this and have a family or move on to other things."

So she returned to finish college, met the man who became her husband, graduated, and then had a child a few weeks later. She was intrigued by the public accounting sector but no one would touch her because she had just had a child. So she pursued the private sector and, "in hindsight, it may have been one of the best things for my career." A few years later, while working on her MBA, Karen got a job with FedEx as a financial analyst. "FedEx was still a young company and rather unstructured with each division like a small business. It was so open to whatever you wanted to create. The company was growing so much." For the first time in her working life, she realized "the kind of opportunities that would be available." And, more important, she realized that she could become an officer. The financial career track was receptive to women who had the qualifications and ambition. Karen became vice president and CFO for FedEx Latin America before moving on to seek entirely new challenges.

Possessing an aptitude for, and majoring in, math or computer science is the ultimate. I haven't known that many women in business with a great aptitude or interest in mathematics or the sciences, but nonetheless all the women who became successful had become quite proficient in computer usage. The importance of math is in possessing not only the ability to work through budgets and financial statements but also the ability to think strategically and solve problems from the most basic to the most intricate. Technologically, the key is to remain adept and current. Staying ahead of Moore's law—that semiconductor transistors will double every couple of years (or why our computers are prehistoric as soon as we get them home from the store)—is essential and impressive. Essential because women need to remain ahead of the curve, to be one step ahead. And impressive because it is least expected of us and we always want to favorably surprise, too.

Today there is a lack of women in technology. Yet, in fact, there has been less discrimination in technology than in many other business disciplines today. Because of the disproportionate number of women tech entrepreneurs, there were, before the great 2000–01 meltdown, more women in higher positions in this industry than in any other. But, even with all the extraordinary growth in the industry, there are still proportionately fewer women in the field overall. A recent study indicated that, "women are underrepresented in most information technology categories, except for data entry—one of the lowest-paid fields, where they are 84 percent of the work force. Women make up 44 percent of all U.S. employees but only 8 percent of electrical engineers and 28 percent of computer systems analysts and scientists."[2]

L. A. Lorek of the *Fort Lauderdale Sun-Sentinel* asked the late Anita Borg, founder of the Institute for Women and Technology at Xerox Corp.'s Palo Alto (California) Research Center, what if only thirty-year-old women developed technology and all of it were geared to thirteen-year-old girls? "Technology would be out of balance, but today, men hold the power and boys drive the market in the technology field," Borg replied. "Women need to take a greater role in creating hardware and software products. The genius of women has not been tapped by this industry. The companies that finally figure out how to tap into that genius are going to eat everyone else's lunch."

The technology companies with female CEOs in the early 2000s were predominantly success story web start-ups. Sadly, the broad percentage of women heading these tech companies, and of women in the industry in general, jibes poorly with recent studies that report that, as a group, women still shun technology, computers, and math.

Jupiter Communications conducted a survey in conjunction with Media Metrix, the web advertising measurement company. The survey, "It's a Woman's World Wide Web," studied the behavior of both sexes on the Web. What they found was quite surprising. For the first time, in the year 2000, "women outnumber men online, with a 50.4 percent share of the online population," as reported in the *New York Times* on August 14, 2000. According to Anya Sacharow, an analyst at Jupiter, "Women are interested in a more efficient experience—getting online and getting off."[3] We are technology enabled. This should make a major difference going forward in this century.

Women are also more adept at "web thinking," according to Helen Fisher in her book, *The First Sex: The Natural Talents of Women and How They Are Changing the World.* Reviewing the book, Catherine Arnst, science staff member of *BusinessWeek,* noted that Fisher "backs up her claim with lots of studies showing that women, more so than men, tend to gather disparate facts, consider all the options, and place issues in a broad context. They are better at long-range planning, can intuit more from verbal cues and body language, and will consider more points of view." "Men," she says, "compartmentalize their attention, focusing on just one thing at a time while tuning out extraneous stimuli."[4]

Fisher labels this straightforward approach "step thinking," which works just fine when all that matters is cranking out widgets. But, she says, "with the growing complexity of the global marketplace, companies will need executives that can assimilate a range of data, embrace ambiguity, and set business objectives within a broader social context—in other words, women executives."[5] Studying math and understanding economics and computer science bolster knowledge for long-term strategy and complex problem solving. This is where women seize muscle in the game. If this is a game. Women are naturally better multitaskers than men. Honing our natural multitasking talents will perfect the mix. We are also gatherers par excellence.

Other studies have mentioned that the reason women don't go on to excel in technology is because at some point they get turned off by geeks and hideous games. According to a report coauthored by Sherry Turkle, "Female students said they were turned off by violent software games and felt the computer world is dominated by adolescent males. Girls said they use computers to communicate to perform specific tasks, while boys have underdeveloped social skills and use computers to play games and 'to fool around'."[6]

The report, from the American Association of University Women (AAUW), released in the spring of 2000, also noted that female students account for only 17 percent of high school students who take the College Board's Advanced Placement exam in computer science to seek college credit. In addition, it claims women earn only 28 percent of the bachelor's degrees in computer science and make up only 20 percent of information technology professionals.

The report contends that the male-dominated computer culture must change in order to attract girls and women to technology. But the fact is that women will have to take the great leap, get into the field, and change it themselves. A grown-up computer industry, as such, will not evolve by itself.

The AAUW report highlights the uncertainties facing young girls in grade school as well as older high school and college women:

> While the female students who were interviewed said they were not told directly that they were not competent in technology, and were not deterred from taking computer classes, that message was transmitted in subtle ways.
>
> When asked to describe a person who was really good with computers, they described a man. In a 1997 survey of 652 college-bound high school students in Silicon Valley, Boston, and Austin, Texas, 50 percent of male and female students said the field of computer science was "geared toward men."

At least today in the sciences the belief that women are possibly incompetent is only subtly implied. As we saw when Judy Schneider, from BPI, Inc., joined Seagram's, after completing her MBA at Columbia and a training program at Banker's Trust to become the first woman ever hired in the treasurer's department as a financial analyst, she was told that because she was a woman she would never be able to move up in the company. In Judy's case there was no subtlety; the remark was blatant.

Carly Fiorina, chairman and CEO of Hewlett-Packard, has stated that the glass ceiling has disappeared for women in technology. She seems to be doing her share and has ensured that Hewlett-Packard exemplify that prognosis by raising the percentage of women in executive positions to 17 percent from 7.6 percent a few years ago. Her strongest competitor for CEO when Lewis Platt stepped down, in 1999, was not a man, but another well-known HP female executive, Ann Livermore.

Carly got the helm, and Livermore got a merged software and services business. She took charge of the combined $14 billion enterprise-computing unit, which was focused on Internet services and at the time was the company's most important growth business. To the outside world she took her loss to Fiorina in stride, or at least appeared to. She has remained with the company.

Although many other companies quote similarly optimistic statistics about women in higher positions, particularly technology companies, the facts are not quite as simple as they appear overall. Women have succeeded in the newer technology and recently departed dot-com companies simply because many of them founded these companies or were on the initial team. They became Silicon Valley CEOs because they created software or systems or Internet usage that no one had ever done before. In some instances, their companies were bought out by Cisco, IBM, Apple, Microsoft, or others, and they became very high-ranking executives at their new company headquarters. They sought out the opportunities they knew would best showcase their own talents and brains. If they weren't going to be offered these positions in an already established company, then they decided to create their own. And in the last few years they have done so in widespread numbers. Not just the Meg Whitmans, and the Geraldine Laybournes, but the Judith Estrins, Ann Winblads, and the Donna Dubinskys (Palm Pilot and Handspring cofounder). And scads more. When the Internet economy returns, bubble or no, women should resurface at or near the top.

Judith Estrin is another paragon for math-/computer-savvy wannabe or oughtabe women. In 1998, she sold her software company, Precept Software Inc., to Cisco Systems and became the senior vice president and chief technology officer at one of the top companies in Silicon Valley. She saw the future of networking years before the LAN (local area network) market even existed. Cisco recognized the value. Before the tech crash, and possibly again in the future, Cisco exemplified technology and Judith was running it. She has since left to join her husband and business partner, Bill Carrico, and returned to her entrepreneurial roots to launch a new technology company.

The success of these tech women undoubtedly confirmed my unscientific research that it really is all in the numbers. And although the success was not guaranteed, it at least allowed women to compete on a level playing field. When the industry rebuilds into the next wave and, hopefully not just a bubble, we have to trust that women who make the effort will be better placed to collect their just rewards. The WEBB women who had a math or engineering background were the best poised to reap whatever benefits Title VII or women's lib offered. They could vie for the same jobs that the rest of us, with liberal arts backgrounds, could not. They have, in fact, an easier time getting in and finding more substantial entry-level jobs. Even in Hollywood. In 2002, Sherry Lansing, Paramount Pictures chairwoman, was formally named the most powerful woman in Hollywood by *The Hollywood Reporter.* She started her career as a grade-school math teacher.

"A woman who really wants to attain a high-level office in the corporate world must be strong and outspoken enough to say she wants to run the business and be a bottom-line employee," according to Ann Fudge, former president of Kraft's Maxwell House and Post divisions, a $2.7 billion business. "This means thinking more in terms of finance and less in terms of the jobs women have historically migrated to, like support staff."[7]

The point is that all these women either knew they had the aptitude or were open enough to take the challenge. The phrase "I didn't have a clue" came up more than half a dozen times. You could say that these successful women, and so many like them, fell into accidental careers. But once they were in the game, it was a steady, upward move. Very difficult, but steady. You get an awful lot of respect from the decision makers if you are on the harder side of the field. It doesn't guarantee success, nothing does, but you do have an upper hand. The perception is that you are more serious, more strategic, perhaps even better qualified, whether that is true or not. In the end, their perception becomes your reality.

NOTES

1. Marguerite Zientara, *Women, Technology and Power: Ten Stars and the History They Made* (New York: Amacom, 1987), p. 19.

2. L. A. Lorek, "Male-dominated Tech Industry Launching Programs to Attract Women," in the *Fort Lauderdale Sun-Sentinel,* April 14, 2000.

3. Laurie J. Flynn, "Internet Is More Than Just Fun for Women," *New York Times*, August 14, 2000.

4. A review of Helen Fisher's book was put forth by Catherine Arnst, in "Will the 21st Century Be a Woman's World?" *BusinessWeek,* June 14, 1999, p. 24.

5. Ibid.

6. The report "Tech-Savvy: Educating Girls in the New Computer Age" was quoted in the *Miami Herald,* April 15, 2000, in an article by Martha Woodall from the Knight Ridder News Service. Sherry Turkle, professor of sociology at the Massachusetts Institute of Technology, cochaired a commission to study women/girls in the technology age.

7. Laura Koss-Feder, "Study Finds Wage Gap Is Just the Beginning," *Women's eNews,* June 17, 2002.

Chapter 4

NICE . . . NOT

If you can't be a good example, then you'll just have to be a horrible warning.

—Catherine Aird

There were many roadblocks on the way up. What we WEBBs needed was a pathfinder or at least a guide. We were all so imbued with warnings about what we couldn't do, or as Gail Sheehy calls it in her 1981 bestseller, *Pathfinders,* "women can't dos,"[1] that we in the WEBB generation became our own gatekeepers. The lucky ones found themselves in a fortuitous situation. For them, the stars were properly aligned with a boss who either needed them at that moment or someone who saw the potential in them. Almost 100 percent of the time the boss was male, and he wasn't confused about his own future. Somewhere along the road, there was that one man in a position of power or influence who either promoted or hired or influenced others to do so that ultimately made a difference in the careers of so many women.

Diane de Vries Ashley, a director of private banking at Bank of America, had more ups and downs than she would have chosen on her career path, but she also had the good fortune to have had one boss who really supported his personally selected staff. When he started a new banking venture, he asked Diane to join him: "If it hadn't been for him, I wouldn't have gotten where I did. He did this for a lot of people. He literally gave me a career."

You need someone. Call it a pathfinder, a role model, a mentor, or an angel. There should be someone you can admire and emulate. Or someone who believes in you. Or maybe just someone whose style infuses itself into your own subconscious and waits for the right time to emerge. By the time it surfaces, you are the one with the great management style and the fast, or at least steady, track. Mary Barneby, president of Delaware Retail Investment Services, commented:

> Role models, if you don't have them, you kind of find them. We had to make ours up. I actually had a man who was my mentor at Merrill Lynch. He never said he was my mentor, but as I look back on it, he was. He was a very young man, the typical Merrill Lynch fast track person. He came from one of the branch offices and was tracked to a very senior position at the firm. Ultimately, he served as vice chairman of the firm and was president of their whole private client business for years. When he came in he was thirty-two or so. I was twenty-two. I loved the way he managed people. I watched the way he was gender blind. He attracted people to work for him who were high energy and enthusiastic, and he had this great way of getting people to work together. He was upbeat and happy. I watched and learned a lot from him. He made work fun. I thought that's what people really needed to be motivated.

Sue Kronick's experience was similar. Without a mandate, without a big deal being made over it, she had her angels in the retail field:

> There were two people early on who gave the most thought to my career: Marvin Traub[2] and Norman Axelrod, who were both very supportive bosses. Norman was a senior vice president/general manager when I was a divisional manager at Bloomingdale's. He was challenging, supportive, and encouraging. Marvin thought about what kind of breadth of experience would be good for me. He wasn't afraid to lose my expertise in one area so I could gain expertise in another. That was a very unusual thing. Today, since jobs are much bigger as companies have become more streamlined, moving someone cross-functionally and laterally is a courageous decision for a boss to make. It is a great way to grow people.

For Liane Hansen, host of *Weekend Edition Sunday* at National Public Radio, it was having someone to give her a boost and show her the ropes: "My angels are Susan Stamberg, Terry Gross, Noah Adams, and Daniel Schorr. Each took the time to tell me I had talent and then how to use it. They also told me what I did wrong, and what I did right."

Having someone who opens doors, at least figuratively, if not literally, is the Rolls-Royce of career aids. Angels or mentors, it doesn't matter as long as it comes from the heart and not just from corporate mandates. Mandates only work so far and help so much. They are better than nothing at all, but staying alert also helps. Identifying those traits you admire in someone else and hope to replicate is helpful as it gives you information that can be very useful to you as you form your own style. Imitation is the sincerest form of flattery; you can pick and choose from the best.

By keeping your eyes open and your ears pointed up you'll get the most and best information, because you can't rely on finding an angel; it is too often rare. According to Chickie Bucco:

> You make your own luck. I went to work at the telephone company in Virginia. I took orders and without knowing it I was getting into sales and started winning prizes. I joined the union and signed up all the clerical workers in Virginia, Maryland and Tennessee. I loved it. By the time I was twenty, I was working four days a week for the telephone company, and one day a week for the union. But without the telephone company I never would have been successful in New York. I worked for a woman who was really tough. She allowed us only two fifteen-minute breaks a day; but that is where I learned responsibility about working. Then I was transferred to New York and ended up doing something totally opposite. Everything I had been doing for the union and the telephone company was sales. I didn't know it was sales. Here they wanted to promote me but I didn't want to be in middle management. I was a union person. And this was a disaster. We were all women on the job.
>
> No one liked me. But indirectly, I found my next move through a woman. I would sit in the lounge and listen to what all the women spoke about. I heard them mention someone who had this same job we had and went to Blair TV. So I figured if she could do it, I could. I still didn't realize I had any sales talent. So I found out which employment agency she went to, that's how we used to do it, and they told me I needed a college degree and to know how to type. I never learned how to type because I didn't want to. But I convinced the woman to just let me get the interview and I'd take it from there.

And she did. Chickie Bucco eventually became vice president, director of marketing sales at KTVG Direct Marketing. She is one of the highest-level women in media representation. And she nurtures everybody.

So does Carolyn Baldwin Byrd, a natural WEBB mentor: "I mentor everyone, black, white, men and women, whatever. Their objective is to find out how I got to the level I did, and secondly how they can reach it too. It is a self-interest. If you can help me, then I'll be there. I want to know what you can do for me, and what you can tell me."

Although women have a natural talent for nurturing that does serve us well in management, we have to be very careful that this nurturing is not seen as nice. Nice is not nurturing. Nice is innocuous and detrimental to our career. What we don't want to be called is nice. Nice is not a compliment in the office. As more women are present in the workplace, there will be more demand made for civility, but nice may not be it. Once when I was at First Boston, Ferrell R. who sat next to me on the international trading desk, told me: "You're too nice for this business." I believe he meant it kindly. But I also knew that deep down he was telling me I wasn't cut out for Wall Street. "Interpersonal skills may be recognized as important, but they aren't explicitly seen as corner-office skills," says Deborah Merrill Sands, codirector of Simmons College Center on Genders & Organization.[3]

As Spencer Humphrey, from Scholastic Inc., realized early on in the game, nice is about the worst thing you can call a woman grappling her way up the ladder:

> Women really have to examine the words they use aloud or internally as nice. Every time you use the word *nice* in an aspirational way, you are shutting off all the very important words that aren't covered by that small, puny, unimportant word. Words like *integrity,* and *loyalty,* and *truthfulness,* and *support,* and big important things a person can be or be described as being, do NOT boil down to nice. We get stuck in nice faster than a speeding bullet. I have had to say to people that I am not. And I do not aspire to be. Nice ain't it. I constantly have to drag my female employees out of nice because they are less productive than they need to be, less important than they need to be, less valuable than they need to be because they are stuck in nice.

Karen Elliott House discovered the same thing, years into her successful career as a *Wall Street Journal* reporter:

> I remember I was covering a story on Earl Butz, the agriculture secretary, when I covered agriculture, and somebody from *People* magazine came along and he went to talk to him, when he was supposed to be talking to me. I was really angry. I wrote a note to my now ex-husband saying that this was outrageous; my philosophy had always been that persistence pays. I had been persisting and here it didn't pay, so clearly you have to conclude that if you want something, ask. The worst thing that can happen is that the answer is no, and being nice won't get it for you.

We have to be very careful about what corporations say and what they mean. That's another benefit of being alert. "Companies may say they want collaborative leaders, but they still hold deep-seated beliefs that top managers need to be heroic figures," Deborah Sands notes. Companies will say they want a balance in management and they appreciate the skills women offer, but, as the *BusinessWeek* article in which Sands was quoted points out, "the rhetoric doesn't always translate."[4]

Changing such a deeply etched mind-set is tough. As long as women are not the ones making the ultimate big decisions, business will continue to play the same tune. Of course, women, as we learned, have to do away with their own prejudices and little jealousies. Karen Elliott House adds:

> In the corporate environment, there was a time, and I think it probably, sadly is still true, when all the women's lib stuff came, and then there was the backlash—you were supposed to conclude that you didn't want to be like Gloria Steinem and Betty Friedan. If you would just be nice and quiet, your talents would be recognized. You didn't want to be a bra-burner, that was the pejorative. Then you discover if you are nice and quiet, nothing comes to you, and if you are a bra-burner you may not get anything either. But you won't get discovered sitting on a park bench in Central Park. It's not going to happen.

Well, here's the dilemma. If we are patsies, it's because we are too intimidated to stand up for our own rights, and we end up being bullied. But if we are assertive, not afraid, and don't cower, then we have all sorts of insults thrown our way.

Doing whatever they have to do to make it seems to work for some women. I know several very successful women in sales who have said they don't take prisoners. They go for the jugular. They learned that from working with salesmen who stole their leads or got in there as a contract was drawn but not yet signed. They learned early on that nice doesn't finish. I like them. But I have a hard time using a strategy like that.

Diane de Vries Ashley remarks, "What gets you ahead is single-minded blindness, that it doesn't matter who you step on. My good fortune is that where I should have had that characteristic and didn't, I did have someone to guide and protect me." Having an angel is the best fortune.

Some companies foster that "get 'em in the gut" type of behavior. These are large corporations that hire scores of women but promote that competitive behavior. You have to be aware that this exists and ask a lot of questions. If you ask other women, they are often open about that kind of corporate culture. Particularly if they don't want you to join. So be alert.

To take the place of angels, many corporations turn to coaches or consultants. Coaching programs have become quite the rage in business. Many women I spoke with praised some of the programs and the management tactics they learned. But along with the valuable programs, there are others that tend to undermine our years of soul searching and struggle in corporate USA. One such program, "Bully Broads," featured in a *New York Times* article,[5] seeks to transform tough executive women into kinder, gentler, more emotional ladies. Yikes.

Women are sent to "Bully Broads" by their companies to work on their "corporate style." They are seen as too tough, too demanding, often intimidating. According to the article, the women are encouraged to cry at meetings and play nice. This is a demeaning message to send women. Clearly, diplomacy on the part of men and women in the business environment is desirable; it makes for more productivity and loyalty in the end. But women have come so far and battled their own self-esteem for so long that to agonize about a possible personality flaw now undermines thirty years of struggle. As Joyce Fletcher, a professor at the Simmons Graduate School of Management in Boston, affirms in the article, women who follow these rules may be perceived as less confident. And as we have learned over the last few decades, self-confidence is our most valuable tool. If it is perceived that we don't have it, we lose our most significant power play.

There are some very nasty people out there—men and women. Until the corporate environment understands that vicious or plain mean behavior is unacceptable, persuading women to become more docile is a no-win tactic for our naturally softer sex.

It just may be, according to some of the women with whom I have spoken, that we really are not cut out to be CEOs. We keep on second-guessing ourselves as to what it takes to get to the top. We change our clothes. We get a new hairstyle. We read book after book. We work harder. We get tougher. We get softer. We don't bond. Out of fear, out of boredom. We make choices. We make wrong choices. We even sometimes make right choices. We are ever seeking ourselves and to renew what we find.

No matter what our final destination is in the workplace, we have to learn when to be nice and when to be not nice. You want to be the one they set the clock to. You don't miss appointments, and if you're going to be delayed, you call. And return all phone calls. Sounds like Mom's advice. She wasn't wrong. You need to be a lady. With class. And that matters wherever you are in your track. And that matters if you are an employee or executive vice president.

Not every smart, hardworking, creative woman will get there. There is also an element of luck—being in the right place, having the right boss and colleagues. But you can influence your luck by weighing opportunities, and most of all by seeking out someone whose guidance you can trust so when opportunities are presented, you have a good head/shoulder/friend off whom you can bounce your great ideas.

Although we may scoff at the thought of having to attend a "bully broad" coaching session, we should always check to see that our fangs are cut short and that we give the same kind and level of consideration that we want now in one way and we wanted then in any way. This is our Golden Rule.

Oh, and as Mom said, "You catch more flies with honey."

NOTES

1. Gail Sheehy, *Pathfinders* (New York: William Morrow & Company), 1981.

2. Former chairman and CEO of Bloomingdale's.

3. Rochelle Sharpe, "As Leaders, Women Rule," *BusinessWeek,* November 20, 2000, p. 80.

4. Ibid.

5. Neela Banerjee, "Some 'Bullies' Seek Ways to Soften Up," *New York Times,* August 10, 2001.

Chapter 5

DON'T HESITATE TO ASK

Confidence, like art, never comes from having all the answers;
it comes from being open to all the questions.
—Earl Gray Stevens

We learn not to be nice, which really means not being a schmo, not being a pushover or a patsy. That doesn't mean you have an invitation to bawl out your employees or give an arrogant reply to a colleague or superior. Because then, you are not only not at all nice, but you will own the bitch moniker. You need to get the information and if being nice means you don't want to call attention to yourself, you can eventually hit a wall. In a competitive environment, you can be sure that at some point someone will hold back on the facts or details you need to know. It's a power play and an effective one. Or you may get wrong information. That is just as bad. If you are alert, you know when either one of those situations may occur. In that case, verify your information with a more reliable source.

It may not always seem proper to ask. It may appear imprudent. It may make you feel stupid, but not doing so is a sure career holdup. Asking, not being afraid to make mistakes, and persevering are the three most-mentioned skills by WEBBs who have been successful. How they learned these skills was often as serendipitous as how they found angels or great jobs.

Most of all, they learned what they needed to know because they had or found the confidence necessary to best exploit those talents. And sometimes, if they got up the courage to ask, for example, and got an answer, not a rebuke, the confidence came all by itself. But it is important to have that confidence. The women who have succeeded are self-confident. And they are easy about their confidence. There is no arrogance, no self-congratulation. If you don't have it, get it. If it was not instilled at home, then find it outside. I mean it. Do whatever it takes: meditation, therapy, counseling. From time immemorial boys got more confidence training at school and at home. For some reason, girls weren't encouraged to have that kind of confidence. Looking pretty seemed to be enough, so we lost out in later years. If you have confidence, then you can go with your gut. Women have good instincts. It could be God-given; it could be Eve's joke on Adam. All of us who have reached any level of success have often looked back and realized that many of our most important decisions were made by gut intuition.

Sheryl Pattek, executive director, Océ Printing, learned how important it is to trust your instincts. Because she has the confidence she is able to leverage her instincts to do the best she can. But what really matters to her is that she can pass this on to the people who work for her:

> I have to tell my staff, "do you think I have done all this before? I haven't." So what it takes is being smart and trusting your instincts. Do what you think is right, trust your instincts. I will let you know if it is wrong. I won't punish you, I won't be all over you. I'll outline for you why this was a wrong decision and what we can learn from it so that the next time you can trust your instincts and make a better decision. We tend to think that our bosses are old and wise. You do things based on your gut.

Listening to your gut, to that inner sense is one of your strongest weapons. "Trust your instincts. If you are always second-guessing yourself, if you are always too busy looking back or looking ahead, you miss the moment. You miss now," says Sue Kronick from Federated.

We develop that strength ourselves, but we often learn it first from our parents. The luckiest women in our WEBB generation had fathers with a strong and valiant respect for their daughters. They believed that in addition to being perfect princesses, their daughters also possessed an unlimited capability to serve in business, law, or medicine. The unlucky among us not only were discouraged from seeking nontraditional paths, but if we were tapped with special gifts in math or language, we were told that they would be fine subjects to teach but there were no jobs for women outside of that. It was smarter to stick with the tried, true, and traditional. Our potential was not to be recognized. The bar was high, and we were not encouraged to push it very far, although many fathers and mothers instinctively encouraged their daughters to push the limits. Then at some point, it became acceptable for all females to achieve, and now it is a matter of course.

Typically, it was either a mother or father who instilled that confidence in their daughters. It still is. Almost every single successful woman was brought up believing that she could do whatever she wanted to do. So I always asked the women I interviewed about who helped, who showed them the light.

Even though Sheryl Pattek at Océ Printing had one of the few working mothers around, it was actually her grandfather who was her guiding force: "My grandfather had come from Eastern Europe through Argentina into the United States. He started his own business and he always instilled in all of us that we could be anything we wanted to be. It was that feeling, that sense of self-worth and the ability to achieve anything you set your mind to."

Sheryl's career path was representative of the WEBB generation. Confidence in her own ability always radiated through, and men in a hiring position gave her a chance because they recognized how smart she was. She was also lucky getting her first job with Mitel. Joining any sort of a tech company was not the norm for a female liberal arts graduate. But it worked for her and for the future of her career. Sheryl was able to hone her skills before joining Digital Equipment, where several divisions vied for her tech training acumen. Of course, training/education is the woman's domain. This is one bailiwick where men feel good about themselves and their openness in hiring women and allowing them to shine. And for fortunate women, it has also been the one company department from which they could catapult to a higher position.

As Anna Rentz, president of Northern Trust Bank for South Florida, grew the bank to become the most profitable in the state, she recognized the problem women have in exercising their self-confidence: "In the business world, women need to develop enough confidence in themselves to be neither too meek nor too obnoxiously assertive. We should be happy for the success of women in superior positions and strong enough to assist those junior to us. Women managers, in particular, need to be confident enough in their own status that they can fully support those who report to them."

Anna's confidence has made her an extraordinary salesperson. She is confident in her good management style and sales ability, and she has no qualms about asking for business: "I don't mind asking people where they bank and why they are not with Northern Trust. Every place I go, I am looking for business. I work to ensure that the reputation of this bank is top-notch. I don't tolerate any kind of laxness when it comes to upholding the standards that we have set."

If your parents didn't instill that confidence, the belief that you were invincible, it doesn't mean that you can't be successful. But it is one more thing to be aware of while you are making your way through the muddle. There is a lot to assess, but if you have all the tools, all the arms, all the knowledge about yourself, it will make your journey that much easier.

The first step we take toward developing a healthy confidence is to ask. Karen Elliott House from the *Wall St. Journal* assumed she "was like everyone else":

I did well academically and did lots of other things nonacademically in college. I went to the *Dallas Morning News,* assuming I was like everyone else. There they actually did have lots of female reporters; one was the lead political reporter—that was inspiring. I discovered before too long that the reason they had a lot of females was that they didn't pay well and women were happy to take the jobs at those salaries. I was happy to have the opportunity, and I lobbied to go to Washington. After a year they sent me to their Washington bureau. I had no idea I wasn't getting paid— $125 a week sounded like a fortune. Money has never been a big issue. That was not my primary motivation. It was a license to learn and a fascinating thing to do.

I went to Washington in October of 1971 and Sarah McClendon from Texas used to cover the White House, Helen Thomas was there for UPI, and another woman named Fran Lewin had just been promoted for AP. I thought it was wonderful, I'm never going to be the first woman to do anything. All the stories in *Ms.* magazine perhaps were just history. I'll just follow it along. But I realized a few years later that people see women as having jobs and men as having careers. So then you started to realize how lucky [you are] to have these opportunities and if anyone needs anything more, they'll ask me. Yes, they'll ask you to do another reporting assignment and then another. But no one is looking at you and thinking you can be more than a reporter. So then I adopted the philosophy if you want something, ask—the worst that can happen is that the answer is no. I just kind of figured that out.

Like Karen, Liane Hansen, host, *Weekend Edition Sunday,* NPR Radio, developed her confidence by putting what she did and who she was into perspective:

The first thing I learned was to do small jobs very well, to perform the tedious tasks enthusiastically. I learned to listen, spending many hours cutting interviews done by Susan Stamberg, and Terry Gross taught me now to conduct an interview. I learned to ask for help. I learned that what we do is only a radio show. I learned to be the same person on the air as I am off the air. I learned how to say no.

Title VII authorized and established the Equal Employment Opportunity Commission (EEOC) to administer and enforce the law. However, the EEOC and Title VII promises were often detrimental to women and ultimately put a lot of pressure on us. We kept silent out of fear of appearing stupid. If we asked a question that some guy thought we ought to know the answer to, we were immediately dubbed EEOC recruits. They assumed that we got our jobs to fill a quota and not because of our capabilities. That feeling of having to do it all alone stayed with us. We didn't need a drill sergeant in boot camp to scream in our faces; we did it by ourselves. That taught us a good lesson: we can ask.

And, we can ask "dumb," as one senior marketing executive counsels:

> In asking a question "dumb," you get a better answer than smart. It kind of startles people. It is important, especially with what I do. I'm trying to figure out how to position a product or a service. I'm looking to get a new angle on it. I have no regret about asking a question "dumb." I'll say I don't really understand anything you are talking about but what is . . . . for example? Most women, in my experience, won't do that. They're afraid. They'll say, "I don't understand it well enough, or I haven't thought it through, or I don't have enough background, I'm going to go research it, or I wouldn't ask a question unless I actually knew that I was asking it in a smart way because I'm going to look dumb." I do. In a room full of men I get away with it, because I am a woman. I'm comfortable breaking the ice and asking the dumb woman's questions. I need to know the answer if I don't understand it.

Although we can ask, for some reason, we are often afraid to and that fear leaves us very vulnerable. If we don't know the answer, we are at a disadvantage in making decisions or taking strategies to a next level. Men ask. Or they get someone to ask for them. They don't agonize about every possible scenario that could occur if they asked a stupid question.

For some of us the traumas of our first years, of coming off the EEOC stigma, were really tough. We know now what we should have done; we needed to get over feeling that if we asked we would be the object of derision or lose the little mound of firm footing we had built up. Carol Aynsley, vice president business development at Medical Dallas City, commented: "The deal is I can't show weakness. I look at it as I'm showing weakness if I stop for support. That is very destructive for women. I work so hard and I have gotten so burned out. And then there is this fear that if I step out, then I'm never going to catch up or I won't be employable."

Consensus among many of the women executives was that Jill Barad's (former CEO of Mattel) overplayed dismissal from Mattel came down to one major flaw. She didn't accept as much help as she should have. And, according to these women, help was offered. Apparently Barad never felt she had gotten the acclaim she deserved for what she had accomplished over the years. When she made it to the top, she was anxious that the same people who had been taking credit away from her over the years might try it again. So she sought to do it all herself, and that ultimately was her undoing as the Mattel board began to withdraw support.

How do we shake the emotion that paralyzes us from asking? If we can't master it, we will surely not survive in today's corporate world. Asking questions when you need to know the answer and asking for help when you need it are critical. They separate triumph from mediocrity.

The WEBBs who really made it to the top are exceptional. They share certain traits that are attributes or perhaps gifts that they have, either instinctively or by selection. They take risks and ask for what they want. They are not afraid to ask now and never were. On their way up they asked for more and better assignments, they asked about money and perks, they asked for help when they were not sure, or even if they were, just to get a consensus. But they made their own decisions. They were not fearful about making decisions. Each one knew that the worst case would be that they would get fired. Nevertheless, they followed their beliefs. There was no concern about making decisions just to please others. "If more women are going to be in senior positions, they're going to fail the way men fail. We just have to have a natural acceptance of that," says Shelly Lazarus, Chair and CEO of Ogilvy & Mather Worldwide.

Most of us don't ask. We don't ask for what we do deserve and never for what we want. We are terrified about asking questions about things to which we don't already know the answer. We often don't even ask what salary we will get in a new job or what the benefits are. And when we do, we come off so hesitant or so aggressive that we lose more than we might have gained.

But as Chickie Bucco from Katz Communications says, "It is easier to ask forgiveness than permission. I would tell girls today: 'don't be so afraid.'"

It helps to understand the macro, the big picture, to ensure that your decisions really fit in the world around you, whether that immediate world is a division, a department, or the entire company. We don't exist in a vacuum even though we often feel that we are out there by ourselves. There are people in a position to help, no matter what the issue. There are experts. All the women advised that we seek out the people with the expertise. Making decisions in isolation is usually not the best way, although for some people it may be the most comfortable.

It is important not only to ask for help but also for jobs or better positions or for a better salary. Few of us ever imagined that we would make a lot of money. That wasn't our prime motivator. Most of the women I spoke with simply wanted temporary financial independence and an interesting life.

Interesting, challenging, good jobs are rarely offered out of nowhere. It's through a headhunter, an ad, the Internet, a friend, or a former colleague or employer. Sometimes a great job is even there for the asking, waiting for you. You just have to have the confidence to ask for it. The worst that can happen is that you won't get it. In fact, we'll see a lot of worst cases that may cause immediate humiliation but surely not lifelong distress. This is what happened to Cheryl Hammond, vice president, general manager, ATT, San Diego:

After being told by an employment agency that I was never going to find work because I couldn't type, I interviewed at Berlitz. Berlitz had just fired everybody in the translation department. They needed a receptionist, someone to deal with customers. The school director told me I had no skills but that she had a good feeling and was going to take a risk and hired me. This was really a good deed. I spoke Spanish, but I didn't have many office skills. She did take a risk with me. I worked there for a few years and learned a lot about the international business in New York because we translated everything. Everything passes across your desk. I was making a pittance but having a lot of fun. I also learned a big lesson. A guy who was over me left; my boss interviewed maybe thirty or forty people. Finally I went to her and said that I could do the job and I think I should have a shot at it. She told me "I was just waiting for you to ask." She stopped interviewing people and I got the job. I learned a really important lesson here—if people don't know you are interested in something, don't assume that they will automatically take you into consideration.

Sometimes you have to ask for everything. That is hard enough to do. It is also hard to know the questions to ask when it comes to what you want beyond the scope of work, that is, the perks. I marvel how some guys can come into a position and immediately set up their club memberships, board memberships, reimbursable expenses. I have very rarely seen a woman do that easily, although I suspect it is more frequent now.

We had already been warned by our parents not to ask about salary or vacation until we were offered the job. Good girls didn't ask, it was impolite. Today the subject often comes up during the first meeting, along with vacation, bonus, and any other perks relevant to the job. It is kind of startling. But the highest-ranking woman officer at a major international rating agency believes we absolutely have to ask if we seek equality. Perhaps not for the entry-level job, but surely for a more senior position or once you have been offered a job:

> When you sit down with your boss, you should be discussing money. Women hate discussing money, they hate discussing compensation. Don't be uncomfortable when you talk to people about that. I have found across the board that women don't ask. In the performance evaluation process, the first thing men come in and talk about is what their compensation going to be. Women always have a tendency to say "money is not that big issue with me, I'll just get paid what I deserve and that's good." They are trusting.

Karen Elliott House noticed some differences, though, in the workplace:

> Now it is socially acceptable to discuss what you want, what works and what doesn't. We are supposed to do performance reviews and there's supposed to be a process for feedback. The whole workplace supposedly has changed from the boss knows best and you do what you are told to giving and listening to employee feedback. So there is some process now that makes it easier to ask. Younger women and men are less reluctant to ask than we were when we were that age. People ask me for things I never would have thought of asking for—all kinds of personal things, more vacation time, more this, can't work past five, putting conditions on things—things I never would have asked for.

Many executive women also mentioned they are noticing a disconcerting trend. Some of the brightest young women are quite determined in their job search; but once the job is theirs, there is a visible change in behavior. They ask questions all right, but usually these questions are about what time they may leave for lunch, how long they work, what the vacation schedule is, and whether they may go to a wedding, a best friend's going away party, or visit with parents. There is something else going on here. On one hand, these women came to the workforce with an excellent education, an availability and a choice of careers, and no discernible discrimination against them. But on the other hand, the drive is different. They rush out the door by 5:30–6 P.M., plastic water bottles in hand.

If you have the confidence, you can go with your gut, and you can ask the questions you need to in order to have the information. "Knowledge *is* power." But you only get it by asking, seeking, researching. As Shelly Lazarus says, "I think you have to be willing to seize opportunity. I don't mean that in a negative or political sense, but when someone asks if you can step up to a challenge, the answer should be, yes, I may not know how, but I am going to try.' I was never afraid to ask anybody for help. You ask because you want to do a good job. In my experience, if you are being asked to do things you don't know how to do, most people will spend a lot of time trying to help you."

Chapter 6

SURVIVING MISTAKES

Freedom is not worth having if it does not include the freedom
to make mistakes.

—Mahatma Gandhi

Not being afraid to make mistakes is the second part of the three work
rules to live by: (1) don't be afraid to ask, (2) don't be afraid to make
mistakes, and (3) do focus and persevere. We learned the importance of
asking questions in the last chapter. Some women figure it out by themselves; others have to hear the advice over and over. The worst that can
happen is that the answer is no. Having the self-assurance to ask questions builds confidence and that's what helps to get you to the executive
suite. Not being afraid to make a mistake is also a confidence builder
because it means you put yourself out, you did your best, you took the
risk. As Lenny Briscoe, the old-timer New York cop on the television
show *Law and Order* once said, "You made a mistake; it's not the end
of the world." Actually, it was the beginning of their world as executives
for the women in our WEBB universe. It catapulted them straight up to
the top. It didn't matter if a woman was creating her own company or
moving up the ranks of a Fortune 500 company; surviving the first mistake was an epiphany.

A lot can happen in a short period of time. Fortunes can be reversed
upward or downward. Such is the nature of the work, especially in the
technology sector in this millennium. In April 2000, at the very begin-

ning of the tech stock market downturn, *Upside Today*[1] announced its "Top Women on the Web" list for the magazine. The recipients were chosen from the winners of the San Francisco Women on the Web (SFWOW) as "Leaders of the Millennium." Each of the women was honored for her achievements and contributions to the Internet. Authors David Bunnell and Dan Selicaro profiled several of the twenty-five award recipients in addition to Ellen Hancock and Judith Estrin mentioned earlier in this book. Few of the women had traditional role models; almost all had fathers who believed their daughters could do whatever they wanted. Several owed their resolve and confidence to grandmothers who were centuries ahead of their times. And others took amazing strength from their children or partners. But all of them believed in taking risks, leaving no stone unturned in the passion to discover, create, and found. They left secure jobs and positions to go after what they believed. As Marney Morris, founder of Animatrix, said: "I drank the Kool-Aid a while ago and started a dot-com company." Morris's comments were echoed by almost every single one of the twenty-five women. For example, Carol Bartz, CEO of Autodesk.com, remarked: "I take risks every day, since that's the nature of doing business in these times of fast change. You get into trouble not taking risks. That leaves you thinking 'what if,' and I'm not that kind of person"; and Donna Dubinsky, co-founder and CEO of Handspring and creator of the PalmPilot, the original handheld computer said: "My biggest risk was embarking on the original PalmPilot project in 1994. Nobody in the world believed in PDAs, and yet they've proven to be a successful new product in the computer business. In 1994, however, it was a 'make-or-break' decision." These are extraordinary women who took big chances at a time when there were more skeptics than believers. They all had tremendous success. Now it is time for the next generation to pipe up and take risks in technology as well as other fields.

Taking risks in business separates winners from others. It is what separates those women who have created the companies that really empowered us from the rest, even if they make it to the top. Because taking risks scares us so, it is often perceived as negative, no matter how serious or important the outcome may be. We avoid taking risks the way we try not to fall on rollerblades. We may be tentative and teetering, but we don't fall. We fear risk not just for what it can do to us today, but what it will do to us tomorrow, next week, and five years from now. And even worse, we fear risk because, if we fail, our greatest fear is that we will lose everything. We won't.

To take a risk is one of the toughest decisions a woman makes in business. We are not, by nature, so adventuresome that we take risks lightly. Even the slightest step can set off the stomach flutters. It helps when we have seen others taking risks, failing, starting again, and succeeding. Or even failing again before the elusive success. That builds character. It also helps when we have support and someone with whom to review what happened if we are unsuccessful.

Nancy, a former CBS producer, and now a therapist, was hired at a local independent television station at the start of her career by one of the top producers in Miami. She had no experience at all, but she was picked for the job because "I had a lot of energy and he could tell that I was sharp." She asked him why he would take such a chance on her, and he told her that he believed in her and "'I have a feeling you'll do fine, but you have to fall on your face a couple of times and then you'll be okay.' And I did." And she did fine.

The thing about having a terrific mentor or angel who is a good role model is that you can pick up the right dynamics, the right stuff, so instinctively you learn how to motivate and how to encourage. Mary Barneby at Delaware Retail Investment Services gained that from her role model at Merrill. More important, he instilled in her the importance of trusting her abilities and taking a chance:

> He was a risk taker—one of the things I learned from him is that if you don't take risks, you don't get things done. He tolerated mistakes. He felt that was how you found successes. Particularly in big organizations, if you don't try, you don't innovate. He had great quantitative and conceptual skills. I learned a lot by watching him manage. He gave me opportunities that others may not have. He trusted me. He would often give me jobs that no one had before so that if it didn't work out he could say that at least we gave her a shot.

How lucky was that?

Anna Rentz came into her own management style and prides herself on the unstinting support she shows her staff: "I think people feel that I support them no matter what. They are allowed to make mistakes if they are trying their best. On occasion, clients have been asked to find another bank if their behavior toward our officers and staff is disrespectful or abusive."

It is drummed into our heads that "a bird in the hand is worth two in the bush." So why push it? Why put ourselves on the line and risk what we already have? Add that sentiment to the others that we were taught, plus our already feeble self-confidence, and it's no wonder we hold back.

I confess that I often enjoyed watching the television show called *Who Wants to Be a Millionaire?* at the beginning of its run. One thing I noticed was the difference in behavior between the male and female contestants. The men were much keener to guess when they *thought* they knew an answer. They would absolutely go with their gut and risk it with the confidence that they have a far greater than 50 percent chance of being correct. And often they would leave lifelines untouched. (In the show format, contestants were allowed three "lifelines"—help from the audience; 50/50, where they picked two of the four possible answers; or a phone call to someone they knew.) Most of the female contestants, every bit as intelligent as the males, did not go for it. They didn't trust their gut; they didn't trust their ability to guess through the answer. Successful women believe in their product, in their intelligence, in their creativity, in their invention or cognitive ability or just plain abilities. They believe in themselves wholeheartedly. They would take the risk and answer the question.

All the women in my universe who reached a very high level in their corporation spoke about taking risks and making mistakes. Taking a risk, without agonizing over a possible mistake, makes a difference:

> Some of the most valuable lessons are from mistakes. If you are not making any mistakes, you are probably not doing a lot. Mistakes only come from action.
>
> You are talking about making mistakes, but you are also talking about building confidence. When you make mistakes and you survive them, that builds confidence. My confidence came from learning how to say no. From being offered to do things that I felt pressure to do from my management but I said no and everything was okay. I was scared it would slow down my career, that they would think less well of me. Maybe they will think I don't want to take the next move, that I'm not aggressive. But if I decided that if I was honest and clear about my reasons, all they could do is disagree. And I would take my shot.

Sue Kronick of Federated didn't make a lot of mistakes nor did she fear the consequences of the well-thought-out chances she did take.

For example, Sue was offered the opportunity to run the 59th Street store at Bloomingdale's in New York: "And at the time, Marvin Traub was the chairman and his office was in the 59th Street store. Everyone knew Bloomingdale's 59th Street was his store. I am very fond of Marvin—but I said no because I would have to go from the eighth floor (where my office would be) to the seventh floor (where his office was) to find out what I thought—because it is *his* store!"

Spencer Humphrey's take is reminiscent of the Gandhi quote at the beginning of this chapter. Her freedom came from letting go of the fear of the consequences: "It comes up a lot. When I realize how many people have such a hard time committing, stepping into the fray, particularly women at a certain moment in their lives. The freedom comes from the ability to make decisions, without feeling as if it is about me. I realized there was no consequence if I failed."

Shelly Lazarus, the top woman in advertising today, understands that the importance of taking chances, of not being afraid to make a mistake, is inexorably linked to the creative process. It is not just an issue of confidence building. Taking chances puts us on the same playing field as any high-level man. What is so detrimental to us is that we hide behind perfection. We go over and over the same thing until we decide that it is perfect and neat and clean and ready for prime time. That is not how ideas are created.

Not all ideas will be adopted or used to build a client base, create an advertising campaign, streamline operations, or motivate employees. Sometimes there will be failures. Everyone, at some point in her career, will experience a failure. Some even an unmitigated disaster. We need to keep the wise words of Winston Churchill in mind: "Success is the ability to go from one failure to another with no loss of enthusiasm."

The highest-ranking woman officer at a major international rating agency found that failures are part of survival but, like Shelly, she was not about to hide in the nitpicking: "It was a matter of survival, hating to fail. I'm not afraid to be wrong, and that's the way I manage. I tell people that the way we are going to learn is by reviewing our failures, and if we don't review the failures, then we tend to make the same mistakes over and over again."

You have to know what you know. You have to believe that your instincts are good and that you have the right stuff to move forward. "I am not afraid to make decisions. I think endemic in American corporations, there is a real fear of making decisions. The fact that I made decisions and my male counterparts did not made the difference, not that I was a woman," Shelly added. If you trust in your instincts, than you can make decisions and know that you are doing the right thing. Anna Rentz says the same thing: "Women in general have better instincts, they are able to juggle a lot of balls."

Multitasking goes hand in hand with success. Not all multitaskers are necessarily successful, but all successful people are multitaskers. And like a successful juggler, all balls stay up in the air, and each ball is as important as the next one. Mary Barneby also noted the comparable strength between multitasking and success:

> I think women have been successful as entrepreneurs because they are multitaskers. And that is so important. Raising capital, raising funding and getting people to get the work done, and pushing it forward. Most people don't have that dynamic. They may be great programmers or good in one particular function as opposed to the women who multitask. I was talking to a woman who runs an Internet start-up. She was telling me that the old-economy man just doesn't get it. Women are used to rolling up their sleeves and doing the work themselves; while a lot of our male colleagues go into a room with seven assistants.

Along with perseverance, the subject of our next chapter and the last of our trilogy of work rules to live by, is an understood obligation to take chances. The women at the top all believe in taking risks, leaving no stone unturned in the passion to discover, create, and found. One mistake is not the end of our world. Mistakes come from action and all that builds confidence in oneself. You are who you are, and chances are that your job is only one part of it. One mistake doesn't undo who you are. If you get fired, go look for another job: "It hurts to be fired, but it is not the worst thing that can happen. You have to recognize that. Is anyone going to fire you for putting forth a loosely formed point of view? No. So, go do it," advises Shelly.

NOTE

1. *Upside Magazine,* news brief, April 17, 2000.

Chapter 7

BLINDERS AND PERSEVERANCE

The four surefire rules for success: Show up, Pay attention, Ask questions, Don't quit.

—Rob Gilbert, Ph.D.

If we get over our fears about asking questions and making mistakes, we come to the real impetus for our success: focus and perseverance. Successful women, as we saw, don't agonize over the small details. Their focus is on the big idea, on creating and changing the status quo. They work hard and long, and they have done so from the first day onward.

Tom Brokaw noted that we "had to get it right the first time." In a *New York Times* op-ed[1] about the 2000 presidential candidates Al Gore and George W. Bush, and their gentleman Cs in college, he aptly commented that we can't ignore that this "binge-drinking, class-cutting party animal" is a "gender-specific condition. I can't name a successful woman in America who muddled through college and then recovered; they had to get it right the first time."

We persevere because we want to get to the top. We know that there has never been any room for redemption for women so we have learned to keep our noses to the ground, and our feet in perpetual motion going forward. It doesn't matter where we start, we can move ahead by focusing on the work and not giving up. We can always find an opportunity. Shelly Lazarus adds:

I was always focused on content. I never paid attention to the young guys trying to get my spot. They were just distractions. The only thing I focused on was getting great work for my clients from Ogilvy, and moving their business ahead; that's all I cared about. Anything else was a distraction and I never paid attention to any of it. Nor did I pay attention to the politics. I didn't even know what was going on or, if I did, I thought it was somebody else's business and that was not the reason I was at the office that day. I kept on doing the same job, trying to do great work for my clients, and the company kept throwing titles at me. I did the same at higher levels. I'm doing the exact same thing today as when I started at Ogilvy, turning out the best work for my clients. Now my clients happen to be CEOs of huge corporations but it's the same task. And I have the same focus today that I always had—on content. I never thought about ambitions. I think people are much too concerned about their careers. Focus on the content and good things will happen if you are in the right company, in the right organization. In most companies, talent does win out.

Even Tiger Woods had to learn how to focus. The golftips website (www.golftips.com) offered an ideal pointer for mastering the art of focusing. This is a particularly poignant piece of advice since the golf course has become the symbol of the great divide between male and female senior executives:

Don't Lose Your Focus

Do you ever allow situations on the golf course to bug you and affect your game? Have you ever gotten upset when someone stepped in your line while putting or played too slow?

These situations may not be fair. However, they are merely facts. If you allow them to get you angry and upset, you will lose your concentration and strokes. Learn to treat everything as a fact without getting emotionally involved. Even Tiger Woods had to learn to ignore cameras clicking in the middle of his back swing. Negative emotions will hinder what you are trying to accomplish. Train your mind that facts are merely facts. Don't let them become an excuse for you losing your focus.

The Zen master would tell us that "what is, is." We need to focus on the work or the issues or whatever else it takes to get us where we want to be. We just need to get our foot in the door as a start. It doesn't matter if we start with a token job. In fact, the token job may be our best opportunity. And once in the door, we do what has to be done to move up. That was the way it was for the WEBBs, and that is the way it still is.

So many of the WEBBs started in a token position. That's the job that is held for a woman. When she leaves, the company hires another woman in her place. This is the job that makes the male executives feel better. It is usually nonthreatening but good enough to appease many activists. It is the job most entry-level women aspire to because it is the most attainable and immediately visible.

At any given time, in any given company, I was the only woman. I got ahead by replacing the woman who held my job beforehand, the token woman's job. She had either left for another position, or become a mother, or burned out. There were never two of us. All the women I spoke with experienced the only-woman-in-the-room syndrome during their career. In fact, even with all the change we have lived through, the woman-alone syndrome survives. The tokenism begun before WEBBs entered the workplace continues to thrive.

Typically, the reason we moved up was because the woman in our new job either left or was fired. Sometimes it also happened when our immediate male boss left the company. We would be given the job on a temporary basis until management found someone to replace us, usually a man with experience. But when the search turned to weeks, then to months, they finally let us keep the job. We were also cheaper, so it reflected well on the bottom line. They could give us that spot, at a minimum salary raise, with promises to make it up if we proved ourselves. We usually did. They usually balked at a raise. It was never smooth or easy, but I don't know of one woman who didn't rise to the task, often to the detriment of other facets of her life.

Call it luck, call it chance, it was also opportunity. Shelly Lazarus saw this as such, without being an opportunist: "I went through a whole period in my career where every time I had a new job, my boss left for some reason within six months. I would then be put in a position to do that person's job while they figured out who was going to replace him, or her."

And as we have seen, Shelly took every challenge and every opportunity and instinctively used them to maximize her career.

What drives our career choices? There is no question that money matters. But money is not the only driver for women ready and able to devote themselves to high-profile careers. Many of us have taken jobs for titles in order to leverage a good position into a better one where the money would make a difference. Money matters, but it doesn't make a miserable job palatable for the long term.

Either because we don't ask or companies don't give it to us or they rationalize enough so that even we believe it, we don't always get the same entry-level pay or raises that our male counterparts get. There are enough studies, as we will see in chapter 12, on the gaps in wage parity to prove our suspicions. And women work harder and longer than others. We have to. We WEBBs always had to work harder than our male counterparts for sure, and harder than other women, if we wanted to succeed.

All the women I spoke with mentioned how hard they have worked. They were not seeking sympathy or accolades. It was a matter of fact. Some were sanguine about it. Some were far more realistic. But at the end, it was with total unanimity that women do work harder. The reasons for it have been enablers for our success.

So many of us were willing to give it our all. Linda Stack, former director of marketing communications for IBM Latin America and currently proprietor of Casa Hermosa, said:

> I always saw myself from early on competing with men and able to do anything that they did. I knew I was smart, as smart as any of the men and therefore could have the same jobs; I did not want to be that woman at home while her husband worked. I am very power driven. I like power and control. So (after three years teaching first grade to children of international business executives in Caracas, Venezuela) I went back to the United States, got my master's, and moved to New York. I fell into advertising but I did assume it would be something consumer driven.

And like the rest, Linda worked hard, very hard: "I always felt that if you worked hard, you were smart, you delivered, you got ahead, and that's how it was for me, whether you were a man or a woman. My success is that I was smarter and worked harder and nothing else. It was my ability to compete in the market."

The highest-ranking woman officer at a major international rating agency figures she made it simply because "I was a stubborn son of a bitch. I was good at what I did."

Nancy, the former CBS TV producer, credits her success to her tenacity. Her sticking to it: "My father gave me a quote that I put on my bulletin board right after college, saying that there will always be someone brighter than you, but it is the person who stays with it and tries harder who will eventually get there. And that's it. Tenacity. Others were brighter and smarter and went to better schools, but I never let it bother me."

Sharon Brown, former Coopers & Lybrand partner, figured that if she was going to be in business she wanted to be the best. There was no point in doing anything if you couldn't master it:

It is important to differentiate yourself within your company. If I was going to be in the profession, then I wanted to immerse myself in the profession. One of the ways to do that was to be part of the Institute (Florida Institute of CPAs), and if you are going to part of the Institute, you are going to be part of the chapter and you are going to go to meetings, and if you are going to do that you are going to be involved; by the time you get involved you are going to be an officer, and if you are going to be an officer, you might as well as be president. Then you are going to sit on the board of governors at the state level. You go to the next level until it just makes sense to be the top. It does not go back to if you are going to be successful then you are going to be president of the Florida Institute of CPAs, but if you are going to do it, you are going to do it right. And you are going to do it the best way and do it all the way. When I became partner of the firm, it was the same thing. It all comes down to, "if I am going to be with this firm I have to be the best, I have to be a partner."

No one who has focus and perseverance gives up. They study, research, practice, gather information or people, and then they plough on. Some have definite goals, others are open to any good opportunity that presents itself. As noted, some just fall into accidental careers that suit them perfectly.

Our hard work should have, by all definitions, taken us exactly where we wanted to go. That is how WEBBs were brought up. If not brought up that way, we picked it up somehow, somewhere. Our assumption was that if we worked hard enough, we would get want we wanted. But this can become an obstacle as well since women are perfectionists in everything we do and agonize over every detail. We do overdo it. We take this quest for the perfect to extremes and get lost in the details rather than tackling the big picture.

You have to believe that when you are near the top, there are others to take care of the smaller details, because worry about minutiae takes away from what you can and do bring to the picture in a higher management position. As we noted, Shelly Lazarus of Ogilvy cautions that our dogged concern about details is ultimately disadvantageous to us in our pursuit of the senior executive title:

Women tend to feel that everything has to be perfect and because of that, it is sometimes hard to get to the big things. They feel that to get to the forest each tree has to be clipped.

Sometimes you have to be willing to stand up and put forth an idea that may not be well formed or thought through, charted, and perfect, but enterprise is messy. New ideas are messy. Little girls are not supposed to be messy. Little girls are supposed to be neat. Boys can be messy. You have to be willing to put up with mess and chaos; not everything can be perfectly disciplined and formed. There is a lot of chaos in new thinking. I think little girls are taught to clean up before they go on to the next thing. You almost have to fight it. There are too many things to do so you have to be willing to put up with disorder. Some things are going to be messy. Let someone else clean it up and you go on to the next big idea.

I remember having a revelation at a certain point in my career, when I started to supervise people. If I had to read something that was going to be presented or passed on to someone else, I knew that if I took the next five hours, I could probably get it from a B to an A—and demoralize the person who wrote it along the way. I could spend all my time doing that. I realized that was not a good use of time, so I made a conscious decision to go with the B, if it was sufficient, for what it needed to do. It took a real will to do that, to understand that everything didn't need to be an A. I had to be able to recognize those things that served their function perfectly well as Bs. I could get more productivity out of my time and I could also motivate my people better.

I have seen a lot of managers put down their people all the time, not because they are putting them down, but because of this unending quest for perfection. What ends up happening is that you de-motivate the same people you want to see succeed.

It is very hard to rise within an organization if people don't want to work for you. You have to be able to motivate and bring people along. You need to recognize that what you do has an impact on the people around you. How you speak and how you behave, what you reward, what you stop, and what you support make a big difference.

The highest-ranking woman officer at a major international rating agency came to the same conclusion. "Sure, I tend to be anal. But I have less time in my position now to sweat the small stuff. I do tend to focus more on the larger issues. The large stuff has more implications, and I am wont to spend the time on the large stuff and make the decisions with regards to that rather than the small stuff. It is easier and less risky to focus on the little things."

For Spencer Humphrey, understanding that you could make a decision without agonizing over every little detail was liberating: "It is a wonderful thing. I used to worry so much about making decisions. You can make a decision and you can act on it and you don't have to know every single thing in order to do it."

There is a choice right here: you can sweat the small stuff and be the best assistant in the department or, once you have learned the basics, you can move on to evaluate the priorities, understand the macro, and create the big ideas. Like any fine artist, you do have to know and understand the basics. Look at the early sketches or paintings by Picasso, Matisse, Monet. Once you have mastered the fundamentals, you can forge ahead and create the masterpiece. No one ever skipped the steps. The better prepared you are and the more knowledge you have acquired, the easier it will be to ease up a bit and go straight to what matters, to the point where your contribution is at its peak.

Ever since Lewis Platt named Carly Fiorina to head Hewlett-Packard, all measures for women executives are made to her success. All of a sudden there was female presence in the generic CEO office, and people took note. Everyone has an opinion about Carly. Every man and woman in business has something to say about her management style, her success, her performance, her personality.

But because Fiorina has made it to such a visible level, it allows men to patronize us (the rest of us) by saying, as one male acquaintance (CEO of a medical software company) once said to me: "Isn't is wonderful that you've [you meaning all women] have made such progress. Just look at Fiorini [sic]." Newsflash: She's not the only one out there. And maybe not even the best. Moreover, as Shelly Lazarus said, "They write about us too much."

WEBBs are sanguine about working hard. They understand that this is not just the price they have to pay but their ace in the hole, too. Sadly, many younger women today are opting out. And that is terrible news for all of us. Several of the women I interviewed were told by younger women in their thirties that our lives are just too chaotic and too intense. That is a sign of trouble for the future. We have to keep our numbers up because that is the only way we will start seeing more of us on top.

When you seek that diversity at the very top, you find that you still have to look pretty hard. The numbers are very clear that although more women continue to enter the workplace for the long haul, incrementally we are making small strides. All the predictions and promises have not materialized as we were led to believe they would in the 1970s. If we walk away now because we are frustrated at not getting that deserved grail of top executive success, we break the momentum. Younger women seeing our frustration need to stay in the competition and work with us so that when they are ready, the sheer number of talented women available for the top slot will ensure they get there. "The reason you don't see more women in top positions is that the numbers aren't big enough yet. You have this enormous talent pool and a very narrow tip. And I think to get more representation at the tip, you have to be represented in the pool. So I think it is just a question of having enough women in the game," believes Lazarus.

Nevertheless, women may move higher and higher and still never get to the top. There is a perception that we may not have the skills. Shelley noted that "it's very hard to get to the top. That's the bare bones truth. To become CEO of an IBM is a very narrow world. I don't think an advertising agency is even of the same difficulty. I do think there are women who don't have a shot at this kind of position, not because they are women but because they don't have the skills. In my experience, talented women get promoted."

Anna Rentz expressed similar thoughts:

> All the signals people send through body language, facial expressions, and changes in tones of voice are clear as can be to many women and utterly ignored by many men, making women much more effective at "hearing" what clients are looking for and, therefore, providing solutions. These highly developed observational skills do not serve us as well in a rough and tough business environment. Our tendency to take personally, to be hurt by, comments made in adversarial or contentious situations can render us less effective than men who can shrug their shoulders and move on. I think many women, myself included, prefer more balance in their lives as contrasted to devoting the extreme amount of one's self that would be essential to compete for CEO status.

Judy Schneider, who did want the top, realized that in a venture capital firm the women, as brilliant as they are, will always be the implementers unless they go out on their own: "The women supported their rainmaker bosses. We became the deliverers, the producers. They got all the glory, the money, the fame. But most women are not rainmakers, are not business generators. We are not on the golf courses. There are some women out there who are not as competent as we are but are generators. But still, they are not rainmakers."

Judy echoes Shelly and Anna in that she also believes there are fields where women may not have all the right skills to succeed:

> Certain jobs and certain businesses are hard for a woman. The women that succeed are the exception rather than the rule, even if there are more now. So now you have two women rather than one or three rather than two. Fighting for the same job. Have we really increased our presence? We had two companies run by females because they were inherited. Another woman didn't even know the other partners were pushing her out. In reality it hasn't changed. But that is also women's fault.

Women have another serious perception issue: we are accused of giving up, of not hanging in there. It isn't easy. We saw earlier that we may not always get the support from above or below as easily as men do. So when the going gets tough, we walk. Well, don't. The women, with skills, who have stuck it out have succeeded. Often. What we have to do is seriously assess the goal to get to the next level. If it means that much, then put on the blinders and go for it.

It is hard work. It is what we do best. And it means taking chances, putting ourselves on the line. The rewards are great. It could be the key to the executive suite. You know—your name on the door, a rug (which actually used to be a Bigelow carpet ad) on the floor. That is what we are striving for, isn't it?

It is like training for a marathon. Anyone can run a marathon. Even if you are only running three miles a day. It takes five months to train, to build up endurance and distance and stamina. But if you follow the plan, do the training, keep the goal to finish in mind, you can do it. It is the same thing as pushing the limits for a career. You start at the bottom but with diligence, hard work, and perseverance you will get far. You may not beat any records, but you can finish; you can make it to the executive suite.

Don't give up. Persevere. How many successful people have you met and marveled at their mediocrity? Chances are they succeeded because they never gave up. They believed they were perfect. It didn't take long for Eileen Marcus, senior vice president and partner at Fleishman-Hillard in Washington, D.C., to notice how sure some of these people are about themselves and how off base they can be but don't know it because they believe they have it all:

> Start looking at all the white elephants in this world—all the buildings that were built improperly, all the open classrooms that kids can't learn in. Think about all these big ideas these visionaries have had. So much of it is bull. And these are guys that walk with a swagger, have the respect of all their peers, they got grant money, were elevated to positions in the community. It was bullshit and everybody bought it. So many parts of our society that don't work were developed along the way by these people who were so important to themselves and so important to their peers because they all believed they were. And so I thought, why couldn't I believe that about myself? My ideas weren't going to bomb as much as some of theirs and that really turned me around.

We women bring all kinds of baggage to the challenge. And ego. Here is a place where we get very anxious. Men don't, strangely enough. We need to heed the ancient Chinese proverb: "The man (or woman) who removes a mountain begins by carrying away small stones."

NOTE

1. Tom Brokaw, "The Gentlemen and Their C's," *New York Times,* April 3, 2000.

Chapter 8

SCRUTINY—UNDER THE MICROSCOPE

I don't mind living in a man's world as long as I can be a woman in it.

—Marilyn Monroe

The WEBB chief executive officers or executive vice presidents or presidents are trailblazers. They are the first generation to have the opportunity to grace those executive suites. As we have seen, they learned to think things through and go with their own instincts. They didn't concoct short-, medium-, and long-term plans; they did what came naturally. They didn't have to attend management seminars and bonding sessions to learn how to think or act. Not one had a set of unwritten rules that others had prepared for them. And most of all they didn't have the pressures of expectations. Their careers were accidental, unplanned and unpredicted. Not being constrained by the expectations of others, whether it was family or colleagues, was powerful for the women who didn't tie their own identity and confidence to what was happening in their business. "I don't try to be someone I'm not. If you like me, fine, if you don't, fine. I'm not going to change who I am. I am asked how I manage to be natural, and I think it is because since I never had any role models, I never had any expectations. I was making it all up as I went along. I was who I was. I didn't have anyone I was supposed to be like. So I never wore those suits, I didn't know," responded Shelly Lazarus when I asked her about some of the traits that differentiated her from other women on a similar level. No one ever imagined that women could move up to such high positions. And since there were no rules, WEBBs did what had to be done and, for them, that led to a successful career path. They were trailblazers by necessity.

The critical difference for women who didn't succeed is that no one ever expected them to make it to the top anyway. There were no expectations and therefore no disappointments, at least externally. None of the women with whom I spoke had experienced a major failure, which in turn empowered them to come back and push ahead. Issues and disappointments came along, but no woman was passed over in a visible, audible way per se, not on the way up. Once these women were on the right track, their move to leadership positions was fairly steady. Where there was discrimination, blatant or subtle, it was nearer the top. Up until then, the women who were moving up did well because they were producing and they were being judged by their results. Until the top. That's where the tip narrows, and it is every man for himself. And woman, be damned.

In the mid to late 1970s, WEBBs in the workforce weren't a threat, just tokens. In the early days all the news about us was upbeat. It was always about the first woman to do this or the first woman to do that.

Just like today.

There may be five hundred CEOs in the Fortune 500, but few get as much scrutiny as Carly Fiorina, the chairman and CEO of Hewlett-Packard. As Shelly Lazarus has suggested, they "write about us too much." Women like Shelly and the six CEOs of Fortune 500 companies are treated like freaks in a circus sideshow. Everyone wants to know everything about them—their lives, their children, their homes, the cars they drive, where they vacation. The women want to be judged by their work—for them it is always and only about results. It never occurred to Shelly that she would become a CEO and the top woman in advertising. She loved what she did and accepted whatever challenge was placed before her; she never saw limits or obstacles.

Shelly and Carly are great stories. The news media are happy to have a handful of female captains of industry who can be used to flaunt the extent of our progress in business.

Carly is the woman to whom all the rest of us are compared. Shortly after she was named CEO, *Forbes* magazine published a cover feature entitled "The Cult of Carly." And the story was entitled "All Carly All the Time."[1] As mentioned earlier, with Carly as CEO of HP, woman are told that there is no more discrimination because men and women are equal in the eyes of the board. We are informed that we have made it.

Shelly has said that to be CEO of IBM is a bigger deal than CEO of an agency. Or, by extension, of a consumer company. Hewlett-Packard surely is close to IBM in CEO visibility. And everything Carly does is reported by the media.

Meg Whitman also gets a lot of press and is a great story, too. eBay is a successful company that managed to buck the great American tech turndown, and it is not IBM or HP so the scrutiny is not as unforgiving. But Meg is often described as "soft-spoken" and "down to earth," which may deflect some of the harsher criticism. When HP did not weather the turndown well, fingers pointed to Carly. Nonetheless, she retained the number one position on the Fortune 500[2] most powerful women's list, and in 2002 that was despite a very ugly proxy fight over her proposed acquisition of Compaq Computer. How the results of this acquisition affect future Fortune 500 most powerful women lists remains to be seen.

On the larger scale, it has become more acceptable for women to be CEOs than ever before. The scrutiny, however, can be unkind. And the criticism is often more personal than generic. The *Fortune* article points out that these women have all had to revisit the same push that got them to where they are. They have been advised to tone down their vigor, to be "less forthright." These women have probably escaped the Bully Broads seminars, but the attacks are still there, just as they are for women who don't make it to CEO. Expecting this feedback is excellent fodder for women getting up in ranks. Advice like that for women is not ex-clusive to CEOs. You know you will be judged, probably harshly. If we remember to always be a lady, with class, we can soften the blow.

This unremitting scrutiny places these women on center stage; that is good and bad. It is good, because the rest of us need to know about these women—who they are, what they have done, and how they did what they did. They become de facto role models for the hundreds of thousands of women working hard to move up. It is why books like this one are written. Yet it is bad because women are once again held to a different standard. When a woman fails, it becomes a *woman* story, a *her* story. She is no longer a business leader, just a woman. Fingers point, her skills are termed inadequate. It is what *she* did wrong. When a man fails, the blame is shared with the rest of his executive committee, some-times the board, or the general economic condition. It could be a cyclical or an untimely excuse. If women are going to make it, they will rack up the successes and failures that men do, too. But since there are still so few of us, the focus on the ones who are there is that much greater.

Betsy Holden, CEO of Kraft Foods, had a different perspective in her long-term goal. She always wanted to be a CEO. In 2000, Holden was appointed chief executive of Kraft, making her second to Carly Fiorina (chairman and CEO of HP) in the size of a business headed by a woman. "When I was in college, I said I really want to run a business and I want to be CEO," Holden said. Although she began her career as a fourth-grade teacher before getting her MBA at Kellogg, Holden, like Linda Stack at IBM, knew early on that she wanted something more, something to combine her creative and analytical strengths. Like the others, she is adamant about being judged only on the outcome of her accomplishments: "Sometimes there's more emphasis put on the fact that you're a woman than results. At the end of the day, it's the results that count."[3]

Anne Mulcahy was named CEO of Xerox a year after Carly. She keeps a low profile and doesn't mind all the "extra publicity that being a female chief executive brings, as long as it is good for the company. But she says there are so few women executives that whether she likes it or not, she is a role model: "There's a role that goes with this that you have to accept and, quite frankly, embrace. I care a lot about the advancement of women in business, and hopefully I can be a champion and a role model."[4]

Anne is cognizant of her role and the role of the other female CEOs. If left to be judged by her successes at Xerox, she hopes to see a change in mind-set so that "she will not still be a rarity in 10 years' time. 'I try not to do a lot of things that focus on my role as a woman executive. I'm much more focused on my role as chief executive of Xerox. That's what's meaningful.'"

Carolyn Baldwin Byrd of GlobalTech always concentrated on the job to be done. Like Shelly Lazarus, she didn't follow a track, either. There was none to follow. So "you take a step at a time, do the best job you can, you grow to the next level. And only through exposure can you even dream of getting to that next level."

We have seen that so many of the women refused to get taken in by the politics around them. An ignorance of political savvy was fairly common in these women. Women would have had little chance of winning in a knockdown political fight. Our trailblazers never shirked from the spotlight when it meant standing up for their convictions and creations. Shelly's mantra was to do great work for her clients. She wasn't alone. Every single woman interviewed for this book said the same. So much emphasis is placed on politics within an organization, games people play. But the women I spoke with just want to do the right thing, by working hard and producing exceptional results. And, like Betsy Holden, they want to be judged by the results they generate as well.

Sue Kronick, vice chair of Federated Department Stores and responsible for all the company's department store divisions, moved up the ranks never assuming that there was any kind of limit or gender bias, favorable or unfavorable. She was ready for the challenge, no matter what it was, and she wanted to be sure that the scrutiny was on what she produced and nothing else:

I wanted to do something that gave me a lot of responsibility. Retailing seemed like a pretty good way in the early 1970s for a woman, in particular, to have a lot of responsibility, if she was good. In general, it took a long time to be a buyer; but if you could deliver powerful results, you could become one quickly. I joined the executive training squad at Bloomingdale's. I loved it. Retailing is an immediate feedback business. You are always getting feedback from the customer; in a lot of businesses you have to wait for the results; here you got them every day. I was very stimulated by it. I discovered in a very visceral way that I was very competitive. That turned my juices on. You did a lot of schlepping at the start. You'd say to yourself, I am a college graduate . . . why am I doing this? In the end, the getting results part of the job was really the turn-on.

At Bloomingdale's in the late 1970s you were on the A team. I really didn't think about what I could do or couldn't do. I never plotted my career. I was always involved with how do I get the best results in the job I was in. I was absorbed and passionate about the "now." I think that helped me get good results and helped me get my career. It just didn't occur to me there was anything I couldn't do. Had I started on the operating side it may have been different. There were a lot of men on that side of the business then, and the culture was somewhat different. Still, the majority of people in the retail business are women, but very few of them at the very top.

I never assumed I couldn't do it. My role models were all men. So many wonderful people gave a lot of good thought to my career. I have had the benefit of that as well as help from, I'm sure, a number of others—unbeknownst to me. If you ask did I have a female role model, the answer is just unfortunately no. It never occurred to me that you couldn't do or be what you wanted.

The scrutiny went beyond the work we WEBBs were doing. We found that what we wore and how we acted would have a strong influence on the women who worked for us directly, indirectly, or in the same company.

When we first started working, we dressed just like our mothers told us to: simple tailored dress or skirt and blouse, low heels; some even wore little hats and white gloves in the earlier days. It was a few years before the uniform was de rigueur: the dark suit, white tailored cotton blouse, bow tie, stockings (of course), and low heels (still). That was it. After your MBA you didn't dare go to an interview dressed any other way. I know, I tried. If you did, you paid your price for not compromising. But we did it because we knew, or perhaps we were told and then knew, that dressing like the men was the only way to be considered serious. If you worked on Wall Street or in most businesses, you were not considered a team player if you dressed to make a statement. Fortunately, that conservatism has moderated. Yet how we dress is a statement of our professional position and is as important as anything else we do for the women we hire.

We should know by now that we cannot thrive or perhaps even survive alone. And if we do, we may just be the last generation to do it. It starts with the simple, little, feminine things we do understand, albeit instinctively. Mary Barneby, president, Delaware Retail Investment Services, told me: "One day I entered the ladies room at Merrill and two women were talking between stalls. One said, 'Do you think it is ok to wear dresses? Mary wears them.' I had just started moving away from those ugly suits and bow ties. I was flattered but thought it was enormous that people watched what you did and wore. I had a sense of obligation to these women who were watching me."

Vanity Fair magazine did a cutting story on Carly Fiorina following the Compaq acquisition.[5] This story no longer addressed Fiorina's tenure in accolades. The gloves were off and employees (on or off the record) spoke up. They used some mighty strong adjectives. One woman summed up her impression of Carly this way: "'I actually met her when she first arrived. I introduced myself to her in the rest room, and she started fixing her hair, even though nothing was out of place. I mean'— and here the woman rolled her eyes—'that tells you everything, doesn't it. Someone who fixes their hair when nothing is wrong with it!'" Fiorina's nickname is "Rock Star" because of her behavior with employees as well as her exceptionally generous executive perks—some real, some rumored. They are watching.

In the workplace, "dress for success" was how you did it. Clearly, that was no guarantee of success, but at least you were in uniform and could be in the starting lineup. In the 1980s, when I started the interview process after receiving my MBA, I didn't own one suit or, in fact, one article of clothing that was appropriate for the grueling task ahead.

For the record, like many women today, I have a hard time with dressing down or casual office dress. That we have come a long way from ill-fitting, uncomfortable suits and shoes for the office is wonderful, but I have heard young women ask how they can differentiate themselves. I always told my employees to dress for the job you want, not the one you have today. It is a concern, and if I were to be starting out now, I would continue to dress professionally and somewhat conservatively. We have so many other issues to deal with in an office situation; dressing professionally makes it one less.

Amy Stripe, managing director at 141 Worldwide Advertising, recounted an experience she had with an employee at an advertising agency: "We had a receptionist who wanted to get ahead. I finally had to tell her I would promote her but she had to dress professionally. Men just understand, genetically, that you have to look the part. Women don't get it. She succeeded because she did have half a brain, but I never would have known it." Dressing properly is all about perception, and the perception that you are a professional will move you in the right direction.

Dressing appropriately, albeit sometimes conservatively, matters. No one will admit to it for a variety of reasons, but as Amy can attest, the mind-set still exists that the sexy broad in tight, low-cut tops is the secretary or receptionist but not the boss. We don't ever want to look back and think the opportunities we were given were suspect. It is disempowering.

Sharon Brown brought up the concern of her MBA group about casual dress. They are:

> concerned that they are losing their status. It took women so long not to have to dress like men. They are concerned that they will lose the ability to be taken seriously. Women between the ages of nineteen and twenty-three have a lot of things to worry about because they have so many options. When you didn't have options, you worried about not having the options; with so many, you worry about having to make decisions.

In the heady 1990s everything that had decorum attached or insinuated was tested and dismissed. But decorum is back. Casual Fridays are waning or subject to considerable alteration. Dressing for success has not gone out the door. It is not the Luddite of fashion recommendations. Look around—at newspapers, magazines, TV news, and business news—everywhere where there are professional or successful women. The women who make it *do* dress appropriately, smartly. They are not wearing haltertops, skintight anything, jeans, or open-toed sandals; they are not visibly braless, with bare legs, or without makeup. A TV sitcom star can get away with a lot more than you can. If you dress for sex, that is what you become; we were not those straitlaced women in dark blue or gray suits with bow ties, but we projected an image that gave us a chance to eventually be what we have become. At least we thought so. Even if, sadly, we came off as sexless.

When WEBBs entered the workforce with the perfect suit, the rules dictated that we dress according to the "Dress For Success" formula popularized in John Molloy's book of the same name. We eventually found our style, which was not rigid but was nowhere near as casual as today. But the bible is back. Kim Johnson Gross and Jeff Stone, in particular, have created the new millennium version of the formula. They have published one for her and one for him, like the old " . . . Success for Men" and " . . . Success for Women." They have entitled their series: Dress Smart for Men and Dress Smart for Women: "It's a steep path to the top, they say, and fashion has little place on that slippery slope."[6] The more things change . . .

The important detail to learn from this is that women are being closely examined. We shouldn't be paranoid about it but everything that we do is observed—how we stand, smile, dress, say hello, greet and work with clients, treat employees, and interact with superiors. First, we are watched by the women we hire or who work in our company or down the hall. And second, there is the intense scrutiny we get from everyone else. These witnesses are usually looking for us to trip up, to do something wrong enough to push us out of contention. They don't want us to feel too sure of ourselves. Their power trip lies in our feeling not quite right, not quite the right stuff. It makes us feel like we'd better look behind us as we walk forward. So if the Fortune 500 Most Powerful Women are seen as a bit harsh, tough, hard around the edges, that is probably exactly how they survived to get them to where they are today.

Knowing about the intense scrutiny, and understanding how it affects women at different times in their career, is fundamental. It's like remembering to stand up straight when you walk into a room. It's really like holding in your stomach when you want to look smashing. Marilyn Monroe probably didn't know much about business, but she knew how to be a lady.

NOTES

1. Quentin Hardy, "All Carly All the Time," *Forbes,* December 13, 1999.

2. *Fortune Magazine,* September 27, 2002. Betsy Holden was named in the second spot and Meg Whitman, third.

3. David Barboza, "Teacher, Cheerleader and C.E.O.," *New York Times,* May 28, May 2000.

4. Dominic Rushe, "Some Blondes Have No Time to Have Fun," *Sunday London Times,* October 20, 2002.

5. Vicky Ward, "The Battle for Hewlett-Packard," *Vanity Fair,* June 2002.

6. Penelope Green, "In Lock Step, Smartly," *New York Times,* November 10, 2002.

Chapter 9

CORPORATE MALFEASANCE 101

I would rather be the man who bought the Brooklyn Bridge than the man who sold it.

—Will Rogers

Never has integrity in the workplace meant so much. At least on the surface. And although women may be weak on the team front, for some reason, we seem to excel in areas of integrity. We might possibly surpass men in this aspect for the exact reasons why we have such a difficult time forming meaningful, strong teams.

The source for contemporary corporate structure is found in the military. This did not hold true for the dot-coms and doesn't for many of today's once highflying tech firms. But the structure of today's industrial, financial, and commodity firms took shape following World War II. The men who came out of the war and went on to run U.S. businesses were schooled in the rule of military law and ranks. They brought this same organization to business. There wasn't then, and still isn't today, room for women in those ranks.

The military bias, which continues even today to follow men into the workplace, creates an uneasiness in bypassing authority or a chain of command. The structure generates a very strong comfort zone, offering protection to those who know how to obey. The same goes for boys' sports teams. They never question the coach. And the same applies to business because that's where these sergeants and lieutenants and college football players ended up. So when they see questionable accounting statements, financial irregularities, or exaggerated travel and expense reports, men won't necessarily do anything about them. They won't think anything is out of the ordinary, if that's what the boss is doing. It becomes acceptable if all the guys do it. Given the opportunity, some men will even figure it is an example to emulate. And when need be, they circle the wagons to keep it all under wraps.

Few women are privy to this information. But several who are are also the new whistle-blowers. It is a lonely endeavor for any woman to take on the solid wall of male correctness. It is also dangerous. Any woman strong enough to blow the whistle knows the consequences. It is a big choice. Two women stand out as whistle-blowers about two of the most heinous corporate acts in the twenty-first century and a third that has changed our world immeasurably.

Sherron S. Watkins, vice president of corporate development at Enron, wrote the famous letter to former CEO Ken Lay about accounting wrongdoings at the company. She later presented testimony to the U.S. Congress about what she had seen in the accounting books. Effectively, Watkins brought to light the house of cards that was Enron. The scandals cost the senior executive group their jobs, one man his life, employees their pensions and shareholders galore their savings. Indeed, if there is any justice, there will be long jail terms and huge fines for all those involved. Watkins did this out of a belief in justice, a love for her company, and a fear of losing all she had devoted in time, energy, and investment.

Sure, there are many men who have taken similar steps. But there are so many more men in the workplace who hide behind the good old boys defense line. Those men who have risked their corporate lives to blow the whistle have done so with little media fanfare. And they have suffered. Watkins was lucky. She retained her position at the company and was not a total pariah. However, she did resign a year later. Of course, few were left in the company by then who could possibly have had anything negative to say.

The second woman to roar about troubles at her company is Cynthia Cooper, who questioned WorldCom's accounts shortly before it crashed into bankruptcy, also leaving employees without savings or jobs and shareholders holding the bag. WorldCom has the honor of being the largest bankruptcy in U.S. financial history.[1] Although the exposed CFO, Scott Sullivan, tried to hinder Cooper's report, she persisted and uncovered the fraud. Cooper remained with the company as vice president for internal audit.

Colleen Rowley is the third woman. Although not in business, her memo to her superiors at the FBI should have warned them about the impending tragedy on September 11, 2001, if only they had paid attention.

Lest we think that women whistle-blowers are an outcome of a new millennium mentality, we witnessed a very bold act by a woman in the early 1990s. Remember when Anita Hill tried to prove that Clarence Thomas was not fit to be a Supreme Court justice? It wasn't about a single lascivious act. It was about a demeanor that would not have been appropriate to the highest court of the nation. The first Bush government vilified Ms. Hill. Republican sycophants and operatives published books and articles in the conservative media calling Ms. Hill everything from an outright liar to a crazed jealous woman. And Clarence Thomas was confirmed. Years later, David Brock a former right-wing conservative proselytizer, came out in his book *Blinded by the Right: The Conscience of an Ex-Conservative*[2] to finally establish what was the truth and what were lies. In brief, Anita Hill did not lie about Justice Thomas's peculiar sexual behavior, including the Long Dong Silver porno flick.

In the eyes of the first Bush government, and some of the media, Anita Hill was laughable and deranged. Clarence Thomas became a Justice of the Supreme Court. Apparently many people knew the truth, but never, until Brock's book was published, did anyone step forward to make it heard.

It seems that these women did what they did because they believed it was the right thing to do. They did not appear to agonize over the possible outcome before taking a stand. They didn't analyze to distraction what they had to do in light of their career. Unfortunately, although each of the women meant well and did do the right thing, it has had little positive outcome in the long run. And time will tell if it ever will, once the grand ballyhoo has passed, whether it is with Enron, WorldCom, or even the FBI.

These women, and many others like them who have not been given credit for anything, learned to "just say no" when their moral principles were at stake. Eileen Marcus, now senior vice president and partner at Fleishman-Hillard, realized that to survive she had to watch and listen and then adapt:

I did what they did but didn't lose the humanity and integrity. How do you know what integrity is if you don't know good from bad, right from wrong? You need to have an understanding of your fellow man to know that. How to be kind, how to help people through tough times? It goes beyond you. I took from them and tried to get my piece of the pie without hurting people. It worked for them so I figured it could work for me in my own way, with integrity.

Countless movies, books, and fiction and nonfiction stories are written about men, at least mostly men, who discard their morals for the sake of money or power. We know of few if any women who have done the same. That doesn't necessarily mean that no woman does it. Linda Wachner, formerly of Warnaco; Martha Stewart; and Rebecca Mark, formerly of Azurix, an Enron company, are names that come to mind. With Martha Stewart, however, you'd be hard-pressed to find many women sacrificing her to the wolves. Most women believe she was treated unfairly and is paying the consequences for strong women everywhere. "Look at Martha Stewart. She did what most people would have done in a heartbeat. Did she put people out of business the way the guys at Enron did? Did she rip off anybody's pension funds? They are crucifying her and it is partly because the world hates strong women," claims Pauline Winick, the former executive vice president of the Miami Heat.

Martha Stewart aside, women seem to have a deeper sense of integrity and a greater respect for business ethics. As more of us move up, this could change. But because we played the "mommies" when the boys played soldiers or shortstop, we may have developed an innate sense of right and wrong. For all the time we spent bringing up our dolls to do the right thing, to play well with others, to be the sweet little girls we were, or weren't—all that time we weren't learning how to steal first base or sock another kid who had the ball or walk off the court or out of the room in a tiff if we didn't like the way the game was going. Time will tell if this paradigm changes as more of us enter the fray, and as we have more access to the kind of information that could bring down a company.

We WEBBs didn't learn on teams. We learned in a kind of isolation where we created our dialogue and made up the rules and family structure from Barbie and Ken to countless, nameless female and male babies and grown-up dolls. So when we were tokens in business, it wasn't all that odd; we were still playing in isolation, without the dolls. As we have seen, the women who have gone on to make it did so by themselves. WEBBs never had a network. Women don't have a solid network today, either, and because we don't fit in to the old boys network, we are not privy to their perks or their wrongdoings. In short, we are not part of the inner sanctum. Chances are that as high as we go, some things will always remain out of reach. Maureen Dowd thinks that "there has been speculation that women are more likely to be whistle-blowers—or tattle-tales when they are little—because they are less likely to be members of the club."[3]

According to Edie Weiner, as reported by Toddi Gutner, "While groups of men often adhere to a code of silence, women aren't as beholden to the network."[4] Ethically, notes Gutner, "by being excluded from the old boys network, they can't be compromised by it, either." But because women are not in the network, "'it tends to be easier for management to discredit or not hear them,' says Lynne Bernabei, a Washington lawyer who represents whistle-blowers," also quoted in the article.

Gutner also mentions Maureen Castaneda, director of foreign exchange at Enron. It was Castaneda "who told authorities that Enron was still shredding documents after its officials were ordered to preserve every piece of paper."

As Maureen Dowd remarked in her column cited earlier, "At Enron, it was men who came up with complex scams showing there was no limit to the question 'How much is enough?' And it was women who raised the simple question, 'Why?'"

The outstanding question is whether, when more women are at the helm in the twenty-first century, these corporate shenanigans will be as rampant as they seem or as we are finding them to be now. Most women today would say that more women will bring more integrity to the corporate structure. Carolyn Baldwin Byrd from GlobalTech Financial noted:

> Ethics and integrity are probably a matter of orientation for women, more so than it is for men. As children—boys learn how to play the game a bit more so they bend the rules, but we have not been trained to do that kind of thing. Men learn how to bend a little bit more, are more flexible on those things and they understand a little bit more than we do that there are no permanent enemies, and no permanent friends, whereas most women carry grudges—you mess with me and I will put you in a category for life. That is how we have been trained. That is basically the way we were brought up.

Men are also more adept at schmoozing. They work their way around with fewer qualms about the not-so-pretty side of doing business. Most women are just not schmoozers. Good businesswomen tend to be more temperate; they play it straight.

Whistle-blowing isn't the only way to manifest our integrity in the workplace. It comes at all levels. Sometimes as odious as some actions might be, they may still be legal. Sometimes you have to go with the flow, even if you disagree. It is not a matter of backing down, giving in, or wimping out. If the majority rules, if the most powerful insist, unless it affects your integrity, not necessarily your pride, then you need to give in and go with it. Sometimes it means being more flexible. According to Carolyn Baldwin Byrd:

> It means turning a blind eye to actions that we may find offensive. Men have a goal, they have an objective. And they would step over their mothers to get it. And in addition to that, they will lie in bed with practically anybody even though before that person may have done something bad to them. They get over that in order to accomplish the objective, the goal. Not women. Although that attitude may be moderating in younger generations, not so much for ours.

Sheryl Pattek at Océ Printing noted early on in her career that men would compete:

> They really did not like each other. There was so much politics; they would stab each other in the back. And then they would go to the golf course or the shows. So much politicking with the guys, I just don't do that stuff. I wasn't one of the good ol' boys. I wasn't their friend. So you were always kind of an outsider looking in a bit. Because of that, you don't make a lot of work-related friends. My staff were my friends, and not necessarily my peers.

And you maintained an integrity simply because you weren't part of the in crowd. Pattek adds:

> I have a very high ethical, moral way of looking at work. I won't be nasty or cruel because at the end of the day you have to look at yourself in the mirror and believe you did the right thing. And that's what I tell my team. I don't care what you do *but* you do the right thing. You never stoop to a low level. It is more innate than anything else.

Men in a position of power do a lot of odd things. And they get away with a lot more. Whether they are condescending or flirting with the secretary, the outcome is always negative for us. They can do that, for example, by permitting the secretary to hand in mediocre work for us, while at the same time, she will go to any length to help him out. Call it trite, but women executives lose on both fronts: our work is done poorly, if at all, and if we object, we are unmercifully maligned. At best they say, "she is a very difficult woman"; read, bitch. Consciously or not, the male boss who has set this up then asks us why we can't get along with other women. It is a vicious circle, which perpetuates the poor female-female work relationship. The secretary or assistant creates an aversion to the very woman who is making it in the workplace and, in turn, reinforces all the negative female behavior stereotypes that powerful men love to expose.

Once these patterns emerge, the game for a woman is over. You can bet she'll be told that she doesn't have what it takes for senior management. Management will say she can't get along with employees. She has reached a dead end and probably will have to accept some sort of compromise. The boss holds the woman to a different standard than her male counterparts so she will either not get a full raise if one was expected, or a title she wanted, or both. Somehow she will have to give up something. Don't get me wrong, this is not always vindictive. If these men thought it through they might realize that they were not approaching the situation with full integrity or justice. It is probably not even planned. It is a defensive stance; it is a natural or innate reaction to a threat. And this is often how some men in positions of power or power-to-be react to women who could at any time be a threat to them. It is part of the discomfort many men have in the presence of smart, capable women.

Today's woman has the confidence (or should), the education, and often the internal corporate mandate, but, as we have seen, still hasn't created the team. The team is not just peers but staff and superiors, too. To move up, she needs her staff to support her. Too often, as noted, her secretary or assistant becomes an obstacle simply because she sees the glitter in the male superiors and not in other women. Such an assistant can be dangerous. Sadly, she doesn't realize how she hinders her own development, if that is what she wants in the long run. By creating problems for her female boss, she loses. That other woman might well have become her staunchest champion. This same secretary, to a male boss, will take the rap. She is the one who hides his indiscretions, be they financial or personal. She often has access to his most personal records, checkbooks, travel and expense reports, and private meetings. She is an accomplice. Women on the right track have to be aware of this kind of environment. It is not unique, and it does not bode well for easy advancement.

Almost every woman I spoke with had experienced or observed some bizarre unethical behavior by male bosses. In many cases, they were covered by the über loyal secretaries. But as Baldwin Byrd notes:

> If somebody I trusted a lot did something to me that was just terrible, I think I could get over it emotionally. But in the past, as a younger person,

I would just erase that person from my memory bank. I wouldn't do any more business with them. I wouldn't hold any grudges, but for me the person did not exist any longer. However, now I could sit and have a conversation with them and deal on a one-on-one basis, understanding their personalities, their shortcomings and weaknesses, and maybe structure a deal around that for the benefit of the goal, because I am an older person, a more mature person now, with hopefully better insight.

Cheryl Hammond spent all of her business career in telecom. She was also grateful for the angels she met along the way who helped her get around some sticky situations:

My boss was doing lots of unethical stuff. But my friend was well positioned with the VP so I turned him in. They were doing everything to hold me back. So I decided to take this bull by the horns. My friend helped me a lot. I would have lost my job. These guys were real sleazeballs, doing all sorts of things. One eventually got fired for running his own business with company equipment.

What has amazed me from Wall Street to Miami Beach to Market Street is how many men have such puny respect for women's acumen or for our ability to understand or assimilate information. So many of these guys still think we are simply dumb broads. They have such little esteem for women that they believe we won't notice when they do something a bit illegal or corrupt or pathetic. This has hardly changed in the last few decades.

A frequently asked question I have heard from many young women is how do you keep your integrity, yet fit into the big picture? And once in the picture, which is hard enough, how do you move beyond being a perfectly distasteful sycophant?

You need to maintain the most unadulterated integrity—as if there were another kind. Preserving one's integrity may sometimes seem like a sure way to lose or to have a lesser hand, but in the long run, it allows us to hold on to all the other important characteristics we need to succeed in business. Our need to uphold the highest integrity protects us in a game that we are not all that adept at winning. Yet. We are starting to make inroads. When New York attorney general Eliot Spitzer investigated Citigroup for conflicts of interest between its equity research and investment banking departments, Citigroup turned to a woman, Sallie L. Krawcheck (once labeled "the last honest analyst"), to head the new business unit that was to include a fully independent equity research department and the private client brokerage operations.

NOTES

1. Catherine Valenti, "The Informers," *ABCNEWS.com,* July 31, 2002.

2. David Brock, *Blinded by the Right: The Conscience of an Ex-Conservative* (New York: Crown, 2002).

3. Maureen Dowd, "Barbie Loves Math," *New York Times,* February 6, 2002.

4. Toddi Gutner, "Blowing Whistles—and Being Ignored," *BusinessWeek,* March 18, 2002.

Chapter 10

CHOICES, OR WHAT'S
A GIRL TO DO?

I have yet to hear a man ask for advice on how to combine marriage and a career.

—Gloria Steinem

We didn't know we had to make choices. We thought we had all the time in the world. But so many of us who started careers found ourselves, in our forties, newlyweds and childless. It wasn't planned quite that way. But then, who knew? Who knew we weren't, individually, an anomaly? It seemed like everyone had kids. But we weren't ready; not today, but some day. One day.

Questioned about marriage, my women interviewees had dissimilar responses. No single pattern emerged. They were married or not, married young or older, some divorced, some mothers, some not. Some married after college, some married and divorced. Others, like myself, married later.

Of the WEBBs interviewed for this book, about one-third were childless, four were single mothers (divorced), one had adopted children, two brought up their husband's children, and some mixed and matched. One, in a long-term relationship (that would be anything more than one year), married in 2003.

For those with children, it meant nothing; for those who didn't care to have children, it also meant nothing; but for those who didn't have children and would have, the publication of *Creating a Life: Professional*

Women and the Quest for Children, by Sylvia Ann Hewlett, created quite a stir.[1] She makes some valid points. The statistics she presents do not make us jump for joy:

> Of ultra-achieving women in corporate America, 49 percent are childless at age forty. Only 19 percent of ultra-achieving men are childless at forty.

> Of high-achieving women under age thirty-five, 55 percent are childless, while only 35 percent of women in this category were childless at this age ten years ago.

> Of high-achieving women in corporate America, 57 percent are unmarried. Only 24 percent of men in this category are unmarried.[2]

What Hewlett has underplayed in her book, though, and this is critical, is that the reason so many successful career women in their forties don't have children is because they haven't found the right man to marry. It is like one of these poor-taste Internet jokes: "a woman needs the right atmosphere to have sex, a man needs a place." By the time a successful woman reaches her forties, she is not about to settle for the sake of being married. She has long since passed that stage. She seeks more than a being a Mrs.

Not all my friends or colleagues wanted to be mothers. But for those of us who did, who expected it, who never in a million years expected not to have children, life has dealt us a mighty surprise. We certainly couldn't spend our thirties pining away because the clock was ticking. We already had to contend with the Harvard-Yale study that guaranteed that if we weren't married by thirty-five, it was curtains for us. Our assumption, although not always borne out, was that when we met the right man, we would marry and we would have children. But often the very same drive that didn't push us toward marriage in college or graduate school also didn't push us into marrying for the sake of it. We chose to give different meaning to our lives. And women today continue to do the same thing, even though they also continue to be pressured into early marriage and motherhood (but not as early as women were during the 1970s or 1980s). Key, though, is that we never thought career and children would become mutually exclusive.

"I always wanted to have children and never realized that the pursuit of my career would get in the way of me having them at a much younger age than I ended up having them. I had my first baby at thirty-eight and my second at forty-two," said Susan Perkins, health-care analyst at Provident Investment Counsel in Pasadena. "I am not sure that putting off having kids is a conscious choice. I think it is a life path that you pursue that has consequences and you don't necessarily know what those consequences are until you reach a certain point in your life."

Let's go back to the Harvard-Yale study of the 1980s—the study that started a panic. Years before Hewitt's damning recap in 2002, which for us was already too late, *Newsweek* published an article detailing a Harvard-Yale study entitled "Marriage Patterns in the United States," which promised doom to all us single women of a certain age, particularly attractive women with good careers and education.[3] The study, like Hewitt's book, received major media coverage. It was headlined in every daily and on every TV and radio talk show. The odds against us were so steep that by the age of forty we were probably more likely to win the powerball lottery, which for many of us at that time might not have been a tragic alternative.

At the time the *Newsweek* article was published though, the numbers had not been fully substantiated. In her book *Backlash,* Susan Faludi commented that, in truth, "If anyone faced a shortage of potential spouses, it was men in the prime marrying year: between the ages of twenty-four and thirty-four, there were 119 single men for every hundred single women."[4]

At least one study and even the census bureau data (on which the article was based), available several months later, patently disputed the Harvard-Yale results. Even so, the *Newsweek* lead writer didn't refute the earlier story because, according to her and quoted in Faludi's book, "We all knew this was happening before that study came out. The study summarized impressions we already had."[5] When the census bureau analyst completed and published her full study, it got lost somewhere in a maze of trendier news stories.

Well, this threw me and all my friends for a loop. It was the 1980s, the recession was keeping us down, our government was advocating that we remain at home barefoot and pregnant, and now we learned we would probably never marry. Deep down we all had believed that out there somewhere was our perfect match—the perfect guy who would support our need for intellectual, emotional, and professional fulfillment. Before the *Newsweek* bombshell, we figured it was just a matter of time until we met Mr. Right and did what our mothers prayed every day we would do. Suddenly, our dreams were shattered.

It wasn't enough that *Newsweek* devoted a cover story to this nonsense, but even the venerable *New York Times* assigned a writer to produce a similar story. And, according to Faludi, the *Times* didn't even give a line to the census bureau report, even though the Harvard-Yale study had already been discredited. Faludi attributes the burying of the substantiated story to human nature, enhanced by the media. It is easier to give short shrift to a follow-up story with a more truthful rendition when it refutes an earlier-published headline story.

Not only were we not going to marry but it was that old biological clock threat. If the meanness and isolation of the corporate world didn't get us to quit, fears about losing time on that clock were sure to get a rise out of us. Of course we were scared. Were the choices we were making then going to change our lives forever? Yes. And they did.

No one talks about the now-disputed Harvard-Yale study anymore. I married after the age of thirty-five, as did many of my friends and colleagues. The biggest problem for a smart successful woman was/is finding a man who was/is not intimidated by her brains and/or success. Let's face it, men don't make passes at girls who wear glasses. And let's debunk the platitudes and clichés that so many successful men spew forth. They don't marry—they probably don't even date—the over-achiever, or even the achiever. They marry young the first time and young the second. Trophy wives are not an invention of female corporate executives.

True to the cyclical nature of our universe, it took seventeen years to awaken us again with a tidal wave. Except now, although you might marry at forty, you can forget about a family, because the same demons that kept you from marrying, now keep you from having children. And the generations under siege are newer and younger.

A year before Sylvia Ann Hewlett's book was published, Madelyn Cain published *The Childless Revolution*.[6] Cain, an actress by profession, divides women without children into categories: those who choose to be childless for one reason or another, those who cannot conceive, and those who are childless by chance or what she calls "childless-by-happenstance." The happenstance group is the one on which Hewlett focuses.

Hewlett's thesis in a nutshell is that if you don't heed and take very seriously the ol' biological clock thing, you will find that when you decide to have children, it will be too late. So she advises that you have your family in your twenties when your hormones are at their strongest and then continue with your career. She asserts that, "at midlife, between a third and a half of all successful career women in the United States do not have children."[7] And will not. And although we may look younger, thanks to Botox, and little nips and tucks, our ability to con-ceive children starts dropping in our late twenties, hits lows at thirty-five, and is gone by the age of forty. That magical, pivotal thirty-five again. While we can make no claims regarding fertility in our forties, we can say with some assuredness that finding a suitable partner in a woman's thirties or forties is still quite feasible.

Sylvia Ann Hewlett's book is disturbing because it scares and creates a panic with no achievable solution at hand. This is the 1986 *Newsweek* study redux. Yet, although she seems to comprehend the issues that women have to face—"At the end of the day, women simply want the choices in love and work that men take for granted. Instead, they operate in a society where motherhood carries enormous economic penalties"— she loses the big picture. Knowing this, one gets the impression that Ms. Hewlett is pushing the marriage button for all young, single women with a certain amount of urgency. And if they follow her advice, they may just end up having trashed their careers and being single mothers after they divorce the guys they married to ensure timely fertilization of the precious eggs. Women have been doing that long before she wrote her book, proving how mistaken that advice can be. At least when it came from Mom, there was maternal love behind the pressure tactic. And, unforgivingly, Hewlett is creating a cyclical panic, similar to the one we saw with the Harvard-Yale report. Ironically, David Bloom of the infamous Harvard-Yale report had already predicted that "30 percent of all female managers will wind up childless."[8]

That being said, if fifty is the new thirty, why can't we have our kids then? Or as Pauline Winick, former executive director of the Miami Heat and currently vice president at Florida International University, contends: "they made all these strides in medicine, but they still haven't figured out how to extend a woman's fertility."

Let's say we get beyond all the panic. We shut off the alarms, down our last Xanax, and decide to have children. Then what? What is it like for mothers moving up the corporate ladder? How they manage their children is one thing. How they manage their careers is another.

Let's face it, we are in a major pickle. A pickle that hasn't changed much in decades. Despite all the efforts by major corporations to make it easier for women to raise children and for men to take parental leave time, it's a predicament. Not so much for men. But then, men can't bear children. So until that happens, we have to think long and hard and make choices perhaps at the wrong times in our lives or with only part of the information at hand. We can legislate all we want, but we also have to remember that perception is reality. If we are not there at a critical moment, or we are gone for several days, several times, the perception will always be that we have chosen motherhood over absolute career success. That will not change.

For many WEBBs, not having children was not a conscious decision or at least not given all that much thought. Life took its course, and these WEBBs followed their most desirable path. Sharon Brown at the University of Miami never really thought about it: "we didn't have children, I don't know whether it was ever really a conscious decision but it was one of these things that didn't quite fit. Younger people today are thinking more about planning. We didn't. We just kept thinking it was not the time. I don't regret it and don't think about it."

Sue Kronick, on the other had, realized early on that it was all about choosing what you want from your life:

> I grew up in the 1970s when there was a lot of talk about women having it all. I figured out early on that I could have it but not necessarily be happy. I wired it up that happiness was about choosing. That if I could get to make some choices, then what I would be doing would be my choice as opposed to feeling guilty and torn. And part of it was just luck, I didn't meet the man I fell in love with until I was in my thirties. I really didn't think I could be a good mother and do this at the same time. I chose. Some women can. You can't have it all and men can't either. I know zillions of men who would prefer to spend more time with their children and their families than they do. I think it is a human thing. The world is moving faster. Nothing more is getting done, just the pace has ratcheted up. There is just less time and men are equally affected by it. There is emotional pressure that the okayness of the family depends on me. There is an emotional toll that comes with that.

It is unfortunate that these nonmothers have not brought children into this world. These women are among the smartest. They have experiences to share and advice to offer. And many of us might have produced some pretty good additions to this world.

We are constantly faced with choices. First we need to choose for ourselves. Then choose again with a partner. The decisions we make are life altering, unlike anything else we may choose or decide on from that moment on.

Sadly, motherhood and career is one area where WEBBs haven't always offered the best counsel. Those of us lucky enough to have children have not always handled the life versus work stress level all that well. At least not well enough to impress the women following in our footsteps. Already it is obvious from the footprints we have left that our younger wards are taking a different path. Many are not looking to change the world. They will work for as long as it suits them, drop out to raise a family, and return with fewer expectations than the earlier

WEBB generation. The choice is simple for them: kids or career. Mary Barneby of the Delaware Retail Investment Services observes:

> Young women who have educational credentials, the role models and even the guidance are not staying with it. I know of a talented young woman who is thirty-seven and was on a very successful track in the financial industry for a number of years after she graduated from college. She got married and even before she had kids she stopped working. It was very surprising to me. And she really doesn't have any interest in working in business today. She has two small children, is very happy being a mother, but she has put her energy into being a mother and supporting her husband's career.
>
> I have thirty-five- to forty-year-old men working for me, and most of their wives stay at home. I find it surprising. I almost think there was this push we took. One day my friend's daughter said to me: "your life is just too frenetic, I wouldn't want it." And I wonder if because we were trailblazing, we were in an extreme position, and maybe because we didn't feel we had a choice we had to keep going. Whereas today, particularly women, more than men, believe they have the choice. If we want to become a CEO of a company we can do it, if we want to stay at home, have kids, work part time, we can do that too. Maybe we didn't have those choices. We either bought into the corporate thing or we didn't. There weren't any shades of gray. There wasn't the tolerance in the organization for different lifestyles. I think a lot of that will be changed in the new economy. We don't know how even big companies in the future will look at workers from the standpoint of flexibility, lifestyle, values, and all those things that are really changing.

In academia the stakes are just as high and the choice unfriendly at best. Jennifer, a professor at a university in California, was told to choose: mommy track or tenure track. Decades ago academia and parenthood were an ideal mix. Could this be an even more negative reversal?

The mommy track is not an option. Whether or not you plan to have children as you work your way up in business or academia or government is only *your* concern. Men don't have to declare their intentions, and neither should women. How you choose to balance motherhood and career is crucial. But it is your decision as long as you do the right thing for you, for your family, and for your career. Once a company puts you on the mommy track, you can kiss your future good-bye. You won't be considered part of the decision-making arm of the corporation. For sure, no one will work with you to map out your career. Your marriage and motherhood plans are yours alone to protect.

Fortunately, there are enough women who have made it and have children. It hasn't always been easy for them, but they have some secrets to share that allowed them to get where they are, relatively unscathed. Chickie Bucco, vice president, director of marketing sales, KTVG Direct Marketing, beamed:

> I just loved my child. And I arranged my life so that it was him and work. I let other things go, because nobody is really a superwoman. But I couldn't wait to go back to work. I never had any doubt and my kid is well adjusted. The mother is happy, the kid is happy. . . . I never wanted to get into management because when I was selling it was like my own little company. I had freedom. I never missed a play at school; sometimes I could pick him up, whatever I had to do. I got to work real early. A few years later, when I was promoted, they handed me the list of management meetings—and they were on weekends and on Halloween. These guys didn't have families. But once they started having families, they began to miss more time at work than I did myself. I was so happy with the choices I made. My son is a good example of what can happen with a working mother. We were both happy.

Another senior corporate executive had a similar experience. She started out "wanting to be a wife and a mother":

> I never had a career plan. I never wanted to be running a worldwide company. I never wanted to be anything. I was just having a good time. People said "oh you made this big decision to go back to work after you had a child." It wasn't that I was driven to pursue a career or decided that I wanted to be a working mother. I missed work. I loved it. So I just kept on. I had my children, no pressure to stay home. I'm married now for 30 years. My husband's expectation was what mine was—he'd be a professional, we'd move to the suburbs, I'd raise children. I was so happy doing what I was doing. It never occurred to either one of us that I would stop.

Most women agreed that the only way to make it work was to just do it. And they did what they had to do to be there for their kids. But Eileen Marcus, now senior vice president and partner at Fleishman-Hillard in Washington, D.C., told her employers straight out that she had children and would need to be there for them:

> To be with my children, I just left work. I just told them. You make a commitment to have children, in my mind, you have to be a mother. I left work and I was there for them, for their plays, for their honors, for their graduation. The hardest problem for me and for them was the after-school

program. On a normal day there was no soccer mom to take them; this was the hardest part to arrange with other mothers, because I still had to carpool. So they suffered a lot from not being able to do after-school activities. I had a housekeeper at home as soon as I could afford it, even for a few hours in the afternoon until I got home. Even as little kids they stayed in after-school programs. They would stay there until 6 or 7 P.M. when I got there. And if you were late, the school would charge you $10/ hour. It was hard. They couldn't do Scouts, they couldn't do after-school sports because I wasn't able to take them during the day. But, if there were programs, I would leave. It didn't hamper my career because I worked for nice people. It was early in my career. But I told them when I was hired that there would be times when I would have to leave for my children's programs. I would be going and if that was a problem they shouldn't hire me. They said ok—and it was ok. I told them up front.

Michelle Smith had a totally different experience, one that made her long wait for motherhood even more unkind, in retrospect:

My first experience with the corporate prejudice against motherhood happened when I was four months pregnant. It had taken eight years to get pregnant because I waited so long, trying to establish a career. I had always planned to continue to work. My mother worked. Although I hated it as a child, by then I had the utmost respect for what she accomplished in her generation.

At that time, I was recently downsized from Citibank and knocking on doors looking for a job. I had a brand-name background—BBDO Advertising, HJ Heinz, Merrill Lynch, an MBA in Finance from Stern School of Business at NYU. The looks on the faces of potential employers was priceless. But even more surprising was the reaction of women. The men tried to be subtle. I had to work to support my child. Staying at home wasn't an option.

In doing the research for *Creating a Life,* Hewlett asked her interviewees what policies would work for them. They listed several: time banks, career breaks, restructured retirement plans, reduced-hours careers. Those policies may help to keep these valuable women in the workforce, but they still may not help women retain their track momentum or professional image.

Unless a career offers a certain flexibility, beyond the legal ramifications and employee manual edicts, there is virtually no way a woman taking maternity leave can attain professional parity. As Steph, an almost thirty-year-old newlywed says, "Having children is not compatible with a career. If you stop to have a child, your job will not wait for you.

Someone has to do it and they can't wait until you return." It definitely will make a difference in the long run.

Steph is right. "'Firms aren't so quick to bring a woman's pay up when she returns from a leave of absence,'" said John A. Dantico, a Chicago compensation consultant and a member of the compensation and benefits committee of the Society for Human Resource Management in Alexandria, Va.

"'And leaving the work force can hurt a professional woman's career more than a nonprofessional's,' according to Heather Boushey, an economist at the Economic Policy Institute, a Washington think tank. Leaving the work force for any period of time can be more of a derailment for higher-paid women." She cautions that "it is also up to individual firms to rethink the way they handle work/life issues, so that women's careers are not unfairly hindered."[9]

Boushey feels that the U.S. government should provide more support. And they do on the lower levels where the issue is more concrete and the job is in the office. Although the Family and Medical Leave Act (FMLA) of 1993 does its best to offer some protection for working families, perceptions still can't be legislated.

Where you work is important. Not every company is parent-friendly. The FMLA decreed that employees should be able to balance work and family needs by taking unpaid leave for valid reasons, for a short period of time. The act, when and where applicable, is explicit. It helps employees, male and female, take the necessary time to care for newborns, children, and elderly or ill parents. It covers adoption and sickness. By law, the employee is entitled to the same or equivalent job she or he left with the same pay, benefits, and responsibilities.

The law only applies to companies with fifty or more employees. So we are more or less covered—more if we work in a large company, less or not at all in a small company. But that doesn't solve anything. We can take the time, but how each company or executive within the company personally responds to the law differs. So under the law there is protection, but no woman can rely on that helping her career track. It is a very personal thing. It takes research, asking others how actually availing oneself of the FMLA reads in the executive suite. Choosing a company with more than fifty employees should be consideration number one if you are planning to have children in the short term. If you are in senior management contention, you will have to look this over carefully.

Many women I spoke with chose their companies well. They did what they had to do to ensure that their children were not left to fend for themselves. Some had supportive bosses; others like Michelle, who worked on Wall Street, were not so lucky:

I did not let my son interfere with work. And I came in early, didn't take lunches, left at 5 in time to pick him up by the time after-school care ended, and worked at night. I missed school trips, performances. I called in sick not to miss visiting day at camp. I snuck out to have conferences with teachers. By way of comparison, it was perfectly acceptable for my peer fathers, all family men, to work from 9–5 and schedule time to catch their kids' games. I was lucky that I had a lady at home caring for my mother so I could work if Benjamin was home sick. Most do not have the luxury of a spare body. After school, I missed a few practices but all weekend is devoted to sports, birthday parties and religious school, food shopping and dry cleaning.

Did it hurt Benjamin? Yes. He needed more time with me. Not quality time, but dull, boring repetitive time. Caregivers do not provide the discipline and consistency of a parent. They want the kid to like them so they can keep their job.

At first, Karen, former CFO of FedEx Latin America, tried to hide the fact that she had a newborn son. She was sure that no one would hire her knowing that:

Chris was born three days after I graduated from college. In hindsight I tried to interview for jobs too soon. The accounting firms were on campus a couple of weeks later and I met with several of them. I looked tired and ill-prepared. After a disappointing experience with accounting firms, I retracted and repositioned, taking a little time off then looking at industry. Whether or not it was true, I think I convinced myself that Public Accounting didn't want a new mother. Consequently over the years I believe I overcompensated for motherhood, trying to make my situation transparent to employers. I never used Chris as an excuse. I traveled. I worked late. I volunteered for more. Initially I was married and it wasn't so difficult. When I became a single mother, it was harder on both of us. Chris spent long days with sitters. For years I didn't buy a VCR so I could bribe him to spend hours at my office (watching movies) while I worked.

Later, as a single mother, Karen learned to juggle motherhood with her profession, but she had a hard time managing the guilt. When she first joined FedEx, her son was very young, but fortunately, she had the help and support of her family that lived nearby. Still it was tough. She didn't want to ask for time off even when her child was ill so she hired a nurse to stay with him. She paid her more than she was making at the time:

Over the years I became a bit more relaxed at motherhood, and Chris was a "FedEx Child" attending various events and wearing a lot of purple and orange. I attended his school events and stayed home on occasions when he was sick. But it certainly wasn't the same childhood he would have had with an "at home" mom.

I looked at Chris as my business partner in many ways. He had made a lot of sacrifices along the way, allowing me to build my career. He was an easygoing, healthy child. As I succeeded financially I was quite liberal with funds. I felt like he had earned it.

Pauline Winick was also a single mother raising two children:

My daughter always saw a mother who worked. My son didn't like it. Both my kids adapted to having a working mother. I was working in a man's world. My daughter resented it because she had to do so much around the house. She resented that her brother, three and a half years younger, was at home when I made a lot of money at the Heat so she thinks she was raised poorer than he was. Which is true because I was making a great deal of money. I never felt she was shortchanged, but she did. You did what you could.

She loves me, we have a great relationship now, but it worries you and you fear that you screwed up your kid. I had a series of babysitters from hell who didn't show up half the time.

I attended every open house. Once I quit teaching, I always had jobs that afforded me the flexibility. I made each of my kids' open houses until they graduated from high school. They did Brownies, some sports. I was unfortunately a working mom who just worked.

Perhaps the most important secret lies with the man a woman marries. Most of the women interviewed who had children said that without a doubt, having a husband who shares responsibilities in child raising and parenting in general is key to keeping and developing a career. He also needs to be an understanding partner. Sometimes a woman makes a decision about which she is not totally convinced. Every now and then there is a queasy sensation that perhaps she hasn't done the right thing, yet she is unsure about reversing the decision she has made. Knowing that the responsibilities are shared and that the child always has an available parent is comforting to the whole family. Supermoms have been debunked. But supermom / dad can work.

Janet, the public relations executive, waited several years to have her children, after getting married:

I had two sons, the first at thirty-one. I worked immediately after he was born. Part time at the start but full time soon after. My husband got transferred to Florida, and I continued to work for Ruder-Finn, and then I had my second son. I still had one client I represented. I suffered from post-partum depression but knew I had to continue to work. But my success was due to sheer determination, persistence, and an understanding husband who allowed me to build my career. He understood that if I left too junior I would never catch up.

In some cases, men have opted to become househusbands or to work from home. That works. As wonderful as nannies, or these days mannies, in the ideal can be, a parent is usually a better solution. Other successful women are married to men who may either make less money than they do or whose careers are not as significant. Sometimes, a woman's career is really starting to take off. That's what happened with Diane de Vries Ashley: "my husband decided that as my career was moving up, his had plateaued, so we did what made the most sense."

Today, many large and even medium-sized corporations are much more open to working in flex schedules, allowing professionals to work more efficiently at a schedule that works best for them. "Some of it is just the profession you are in," confirms Susan Perkins:

> You get some employers who are more family oriented. They figure professionals will use the time necessary to get the job done and as long as it is done it is no problem.
>
> If I have to see a customer at 2 P.M., it is a problem. What I say to them is just give me enough notice, if at all possible, so I can arrange to be covered. I'm not going to say no I can't see a customer. You do what you need to do and hope your employer understands that. Guys are making more of these decisions than I saw ten years ago. They are much more involved, much more sensitive. They seem to be pretty good with that.

Sheryl Pattek was also able to work out a schedule that fit her professional needs and the demands of motherhood: "After my daughter was born, I wanted to be there with her more. I wanted to reduce hours but also offered to flex—work until 3:30 and leave. No lunch, nothing else. From a productivity standard no one could tell. I did it for five years. And kept on getting more and more responsibility from training education to marketing and strategic planning. I traveled a lot."

Today, Eileen Marcus works with clients who have learned to juggle their high-powered positions with motherhood:

> One of my clients lives in West Virginia. She works for an agency in Washington. She comes in once every few weeks. They don't have a problem with it. We do everything via phone and e-mail. She doesn't work on Tuesdays. She is head of a big national program and her employer is fine with it. She has been doing it for years. It depends on the culture. It depends on where you are. All the people here are in their thirties or

forties with kids. The clients are as understanding if I have to leave because my mother is ill or if I had a child.

Spencer Humphrey, from Scholastic, realized that she and her daughter
"ultimately created a balance that worked out just fine." She had absolute
trust in her daughter who was independent and "figured stuff out. . . . I
was always there for one performance after another. When she was
young, I moved closer to her school."

Eileen's children are now grown, but she gives her own employees
the same leeway and respect that she received. "I have no problem with
my employees who have kids. People don't abuse it. Men and women.
It is just not a problem in the environment I have with my department."

Karen learned a lot from her experience and over time became a
stronger and more respected manager because of it:

> I think there were times that I measured my employees against the stan-
> dard I set. I felt all my employees (male or female) needed to be respon-
> sible and manage their own lives. I also started out believing, perhaps too
> much so, that equal was fair. I didn't feel that I could treat parents any
> differently than nonparents. I later began to realize that treating people
> fairly doesn't always mean treating them equally.
>
> When I first became a manager, none of my employees had children.
> As my role expanded, I began to have employees with children, but it was
> generally weighted more toward clerical positions than professional po-
> sitions. I faced some constraints with clerical positions. But I learned to
> weigh various factors and became a lot more flexible over the years. There
> were many times, in later years, that I pushed employees, especially males,
> out the door at night because it was a child's birthday or other family
> event.
>
> When interviewing people, I never considered children a factor. That
> may have been a result of my own determination to make sure it wasn't.
> When I reflect back on it, I think children provide a balance that is posi-
> tive. I know for myself if it weren't for Chris, my life would have been
> monomaniac. I think I would regret that today.

Sometimes flexibility is more than handling your own career, sometimes it is moving in sync with your husband's career. Liane Hansen
didn't exactly find herself on the mommy track, but following the usual
standard of the times then, she stopped working after her first child was
born:

> My daughter was born three weeks after I left my anchor job on *Weekend
> All Things Considered*. I moved from Washington to New York to be with

my husband. One year later, he was transferred to England. I moved with him and had our son there. I worked part-time for a theater company. When we returned to New York, I worked odd jobs, and freelanced—and actually returned to the air for two weeks as a substitute host for Terry Gross. This was the return—she asked if I could do it, and that reignited my radio career. After one year, my husband was transferred to Washington again so I followed and was asked to go back on the air to fill in. In 1989, I was back full-time as an NPR host. So, did children affect my career long term, no. However, many compromises had to be made.

I waited to go back to work full-time until both children were in elementary school.

And that was just the beginning as Liane and her husband worked out their schedules, their children's schedules and the need for child care:

My hours for the job are Wednesday through Sunday—my husband's workweek is Monday through Friday—which means we needed child care only three days a week. We rarely had time as a full family. Sunday afternoons were dedicated to family time. My husband and I rarely saw each other as a couple unless we arranged a mutually convenient date night. We shared the school play, concert, and so on, duties—one of us was always there. Sometimes my husband saw the play one weekend and I went the next. My days off, Monday and Tuesday, allowed me to chaperone field trips and get somewhat involved with school activities, which was great when they were in the early grades. And we both have regrets about what we missed. Today our grown-up children are asking questions about their "unconventional" upbringing, and I can only hope that it contributed to their sense of independence. Home is a place where they are loved unconditionally and to which they can always return. The time we spent apart made the time we spent together more precious, and that continues today.

In a survey conducted by the Financial Women's Association, 48 percent of respondents said, "there have been improvements in the availability of flexible work schedules in the past three years."[10]

Wendy Elkin, senior vice president at the Nasdaq 100-Open found that she could also arrange her schedule around her children and make it work:

Before I had children I was in at 7:30 and worked until 7:30 every night. That change was huge. I tried different things. When I had my first child, I still worked full-time. When I became pregnant with my twins I went to Butch Buchholz and told him that I had no idea what to expect. I took six weeks maternity with my first child, and I would take three months

maternity leave with the twins, I just didn't know. He said, "whatever you
need, we'll make it work." After two months I was already back on e-
mail and back in the swing of things; I was missing the daily action with
everyone so I came back. I tried different things, Monday, Wednesday,
Friday full days, then Monday, Tuesday, Friday full days—the consistency
wasn't there. It became better for me and my staff if I had definite hours—
9–2:30 every day. And that works. We cram all of it in during those hours
and the rest I work from home.

The hardest part for Wendy was drastically cutting down the travel.
She couldn't be away at all the major tennis tournaments around the
world and still be with her children in any quality fashion:

The big thing for me is not traveling because the day-to-day life of what
the kids are doing—not being involved with that—really tugged at me.
There was a conscious decision. I went to Adam, my boss, and said if
there comes a time when I am not pulling my weight, doing what you
need me to do, let me know because then I'll go. But you need to let me
know. It was a big decision at the time. But now I look back and know
it was the right decision. But some times I miss that I am not in the thick
of it.

Traveling is always a tricky issue. You are either not here or not there.
But for sure, you can't be both places at once. It can make a difference
in doing your job properly or, again, in how you are seen by the client
or your own company. Many women have worked out a plan that is
suitable to them and their employer. There will usually be a compromise
from both sides.

However, according to notes from Deutsche Bank's 7th annual Women
on Wall Street conference "A woman who gives up business travel, training and promotions to spend time with children may sacrifice as much
as $1 million in lost income in her lifetime."[11] Diane de Vries Ashley
confirms that in investment banking, in particular, raising children and
pursuing such a high-powered career really are mutually exclusive:

Investment banking is hopeless. You have to be more on the relationship
side of a bank or at a branch where you can relatively define what you
are doing. A lot of investment banking business depends on people getting
on a plane and just going. The challenge is enormous. If you are willing
to do it, and I know people who have, it's fine; but it would not be my
first choice. There's one person I know who has been pretty successful at

it. She and her husband, a lawyer, were very communicative. But they still had challenges.

Even with a career in high tech, or marketing, it would be the same. If you are not visiting your clients, you will lose in sales. If you are not there, you'll be forgotten when the goodies are passed around. You need to know that and make the tough decisions.

Working on Wall Street, Michelle didn't have an easy time just walking out the door or even asking male superiors for the time, all the time. She figures there must be another way to do it: "The book that needs to be written for the corporate mother is 101 ways to duck out without being caught, so you can catch the soccer finals or the school play. It's ironic that fathers, who catch the game, are lauded as great parents for their participation. In the same position, mothers are derided for being mothers. Taking time off again. Distracted by family responsibilities. Motherhood in the corporation is all smoke and mirrors."

"It is also up to individual firms to rethink the way they handle work/ life issues, so that women's careers are not unfairly hindered," Ms. Boushey, from the Economic Policy Institute, said. The Financial Women's Association survey concurred. Change, like attitude and openness to women's issues has to come from the executive suite. Unless the person at the top says this is important, little changes. "The cold, hard facts would say things are changing but at a very slow pace."[12]

Even as things change, though, women entering the business world today will experience some of the same ramifications that the WEBBs faced. Spencer Humphrey knows that her career was impacted to a degree because she made sure she was always there for her daughter. She didn't see the same thing happen to her male colleagues.

Susan Perkins has come to terms knowing that she cannot be everywhere at once:

> I just make my child my first priority. It is a matter of keeping in the flow of her schedule and showing up for things. And saying "no" to a lot. It is kind of how I have done it. It has set me back in terms of networking, it has set me back in terms of my career. I am not right now pushing for the top slot, I am pushing a little bit more to be a worker bee. Maybe that will change.

Susan lives on the West Coast, which gives her a very early day working with Wall Street hours. She gets into the office at 5 A.M. but leaves by 2 or 3 to pick up her daughter. The only thing she hasn't managed to arrange is sleep. "I never sleep. The biggest thing I fight on no sleep is not being cranky with my kids and being on performance-wise."

Other women had startling reservations when they thought they would continue to work and raise their children. By all standards, Nancy had a very successful career on television. She was highly regarded at CBS News and, with her husband, a reporter, produced the prototype for *48 Hours*. Then she had her daughter:

> I lost that hunger, even though I was up for an on-air job. I preferred to freelance. One day I got a call and was offered a stint through one of my former cameramen to do an *Entertainment Tonight* piece with Andy Garcia—and I said I had to carpool. I realized at that moment that it was time for me to make a change. Something happened. Priorities change. Luckily I had the choice.

So many choices, so little time. As Pauline Winick says, "Women can't have these jobs. You shouldn't kid yourself. Sometimes they make it a challenge and they want to see if women are up to it. So they push it. These girls are going to have to make some important decisions—what career, what kind of life they want. It is totally different than the decisions we had to make."

The upshot is you have to know yourself. You have to know how far you are willing to go. They are not going to name a cloud after you. We make a lot of choices to make it.

NOTES

1. Sylvia Ann Hewlett, *Creating a Life: Professional Women and the Quest for Children* (New York: Talk Miramax Books, 2002).

2. Ibid.

3. "If You Are a Single Woman, Here Are Your Chances of Getting Married," *Newsweek*, June 2, 1986, cited in Faludi, *Backlash: The Undeclared War Against American Women* (New York: Crown, 1991), p. 99.

4. Faludi, *Backlash*, p. 14.

5. Ibid., p. 99.

6. Madelyn Cain, *The Childless Revolution: What It Means to Be Childless Today* (New York: Perseus, 2001).

7. Sylvia Ann Hewlett, "Executive Women and the Myth of Having It All." *Harvard Business Review*, April 2002, pp. 5–11.

8. Faludi, op. cit., p. 105.

9. Caitlin Mollison, "Financial Women Really Paid Less? Data Are Scarce," *American Banker*, May 21, 2002.

10. Ibid.

11. Summary notes from Deutsche Bank's 7th annual Women on Wall St. conference in New York City on October 29, 2001. Panel titled "Money for Women."

12. Mollison, op. cit.

Chapter 11

COOL IT

And if I laugh at any mortal thing,/'Tis that I may not weep.
                                                    —Lord Byron

A fine line exists between a woman eager to move ahead, to get hired, to join a new team, and desperation. If we woman feel desperate, it shows in everything we do, the sound of our voice, the cadence of our speech, the look in our eyes, our facial expressions, and our body language. When it comes to this side of ourselves, we are not good actors because of our emotional makeup. That means we have to take a big long breath, maybe five, before we ask, communicate, defer, question, and sometimes even respond. We need to know when our emotions are getting the best of us and when we need to bring some moderation into our day. It may mean drawing within the lines, not rocking the boat or bucking the system, so we don't go over the edge.

Sometimes someone doesn't like our work. Sometimes they don't like how we handled a situation or dealt with a client. Sometimes the comments are downright spiteful. Definitely unfair. And this can occur when we have worked so hard, were so proud of what we produced.

We have all been through it. The tears so well controlled all of a sudden well up. Before we know it, they are at the corners of our eyes and soon down on our cheeks. I thought I was the only one. The hardest thing for me was to hold it all in until I got home at night. Susan Perkins, health-care analyst at Provident Investment Counsel in Pasadena, told me the same thing.

> I thought it was really, really tough. Wall Street is a tough business, and I think it was tougher being a woman. I was off crying too. There we are, thousands of women crying alone at home on our beds; maybe we should have all been there together. We all thought we were the only ones. There is actual discrimination. It is not phantom. That's probably why I started skydiving. It empowered me. The guys wouldn't have had the balls to do it.

We need something to mitigate the discomfort. I ran the New York Marathon. Other women drink a cup of chamomile tea, or take a walk, or eat a chocolate bar.

Displaying our more vulnerable emotions has happened to all of us, not just on Wall Street. And usually when and where it happens is highly inappropriate. There is not much that can be done to stop it from happening, so the best advice is to be aware that at some point it might. And if you feel a situation might be that time, be sure to have a handkerchief with you in a pocket or wherever it is handy. A handkerchief is faster to whip out and use than a tissue in those little packets that take forever to open and separate when you are teary. Heloise wouldn't give you that tip.

But, barring those inopportune outbursts, getting emotional is not good office behavior. That goes for the tears, losing your temper, and whining. As Dianne Stokely of FedEx cautions:

> There are things I have great difficulty with; one is whining and one is making excuses. I don't want to hear it. I don't want to hear barriers because I feel as though if you are in management and you are worth your salt you're going to have to figure out what it takes to get things done. And for heaven's sake, don't cry. If you have a personal issue or something devastating, I'll cry with you, and I've done it, but when you come crying about the budget that you have and you tear up, I don't have patience for it because that's the thing that keeps you from getting anywhere. You have to argue for what you can, have reasons to justify everything that you want. You take what you have and figure out how you are going to make it work. You don't cry over business, you cry over things worth crying over.

In retrospect, Amy Stripe, managing director at 141 Worldwide, formerly Bates Advertising, knew that she should have asked for help regarding a problem with a major account she directed for the Latin America region:

> When I saw things deteriorating, I should have called the CEO. Men would have done it. I should have gone around local management. But I felt that I was well compensated and should have been able to handle it myself. If I had been a guy I would have been more vociferous about it. A guy would not have gotten as caught up in it as I did. He would not have gotten so emotional. My mother always said I get too emotional. You can't get too emotional. I surely wouldn't put myself in that position again today, I can tell you that. A guy just wouldn't have gotten so involved.

In the end, we are different. We react differently to almost all cues. Far too many of us are overemotional. Most of the rest of us are simply emotional. That is just the way it is. I don't think the Bully Broads we mentioned earlier takes this side of us into consideration.

We do get too involved, and our emotion distracts us from the business core. We get so caught up in everything we do. But we really don't have to imagine every single scenario to make a move. At some point the microstrategizing will drive us crazy and that, in turn, will compromise our credibility. Unfortunately, many of us can't shake the emotion. Perhaps when we learn to ask, we can also ask for help and ease the emotional chains we so easily slip into.

Sharon Brown, now assistant dean at the University of Miami Business School, related how graduate students were questioning how we get along in business emotionally:

> "How is someone able to bring balance into her life, to be in a relationship with someone? Why do women always personalize things while men just seem be able to shrug them off?" [They asked visiting female executives these questions. Another concern they had was whether the speaker had] "ever been frustrated and cried when she had been upset?" [All said yes.] "They know that they have to be strong but they all say they feel their eyes welling up, and although they try to keep it in, a tear rolls down their face."

Each one felt badly about crying and making it personal; and each admitted that she tried to be strong and not even think about it but that sometimes, it just happens.

When you are a token, or in a very demanding profession, you tend to push the feelings aside. You need to know, and it is nice to know, that you are not the only one who gets emotional. It should be comforting. If you have balance in your life, you can defuse much of the pent-up emotion. That's one of the reasons why we join gyms, run marathons, skydive—why we keep on moving.

Unless you are truly a hard-hearted Hannah, you will experience some fears, insecurities, rage, or hurt at least once in your career. But there is one way to mitigate the emotion and that is by keeping a sense of humor.

There's not much original to be said about keeping your sense of humor, but of all the tips or pointers or suggestions offered in this or any other book, humor may be your best defense against whatever comes your way. Throughout your career you will find, at one time or another, terrible bosses, hideous peers, and ungrateful, miserable employees; but they are nothing compared with clients who can be demanding, unreasonable, nasty, miserable, boring, stingy, stupid, unfriendly and cold, self-righteous, threatening, insane, loud, unreachable, vicious, insincere, and two-faced. You get the picture. And when you meet these fellows, male or female, you just have to laugh. Nothing else will get you through it.

Having a sense of humor is not just about telling jokes. Or laughing at jokes. In the workplace, it is being able to laugh at your own mistakes so that they don't overwhelm you. If you can laugh at yourself and your errors, you will put everyone else at ease. That is admirable. And you'll recover much quicker. It helps to put a situation in perspective.

September 11 was a catalytic moment for all the known and obvious reasons and also because it changed many peoples' perspective about work versus life. As one partner in a consulting firm said to me, "I tell people to enjoy today because you don't know what's going to happen tomorrow." That attitude is pervasive. It is sobering and should convince people to put it all into perspective. And laugh about it. No work situation should ever be that drastic. And if it is, on a constant basis, you might want to rethink what you are doing and/or where you are doing it. Not all companies are the same. Fortunately, you have a choice.

Sue Kronick of Federated also recognizes the importance of putting it all into perspective and facing what comes your way with humor:

> My father was a very big influence on me. He has a wonderful sense of humor. I think having a sense of humor is important and often underestimated. If you take yourself too seriously, you are just going to burn people out, burn yourself out, and implode. There are people who thrive on their own seriousness. You need a sense of humor and you need perspective. I think you always do better with balance. At the end of the day,

I am not going to be lying on my deathbed thinking that I got an extra 2 percent increase above plan in 1999. It's not going to matter. You can be urgent and intense and still be self-effacing. When you have humor there's an easier give and take; I think people grow better in that environment.

Successful women have fun with what they are doing, at least 80 percent of the time. If it isn't fun, almost all suggest you should be doing something else. Like trying to build a good relationship, if you are taking all the time to make it work, perhaps you might think of moving on to something less difficult. As a consultant with a top firm believes, "Screw the money, pursue the passion." That's what she did, and she has reaped the professional, emotional, and personal rewards.

Enjoyment of your work is not necessarily always evidenced by a hearty guffaw, although it does feel good, but, rather by a healthy chuckle. You will make mistakes inadvertently. You might say the wrong thing or misunderstand a project. That happens. What matters is whether you get caught up in the anger or frustration, which is bound to be your first reaction, or whether you understand that it can happen, you're human, and you won't do it again. Find the humor in it. Then move on.

Chapter 12

"JUST THE FACTS, MA'AM"

Many of life's failures are people who did not realize how close
they were to success when they gave up.
—Thomas A. Edison

The statistics speak for themselves. Women have made remarkable
strides in business and the trend is upward, if for no other reason than
there are more of us in the game. Yet, for every upbeat commentary we
read, there are some gloomy predictions.

For example, when Catalyst released the results of its 2002 survey of
executive and high-earning corporate women, the "percentage gains were
so small as to seem inconsequential," according to the *New York Times*
report. But true to the good news/bad news pattern, the happy news is
that the gains were "achieved during a recession, when many businesses
were cutting back."[1] Of course, if we were cynical, we might say that
keeping us on the payroll makes good corporate sense for the long term,
since, even in the higher ranks, women earn less money, and in tight
times like the early 2000s, women are less apt to viciously attempt to
seize the CEO position. In the past, though, women have usually been
the first to get cut in a corporate downsizing.

Today, the concern is about executive positions. But the real test is
tomorrow, as the current crop of women middle managers should be next
in line for those coveted executive positions and younger women should
be filling their positions. This scenario is cause for great consternation

since fewer women are pursuing MBAs—only 29 percent of students in top-tier business schools are women, more or less unchanged in the last ten years. At the same time, enrollment in top medical and law schools have seen a sizable increase to 44 *percent* in top-tier med schools and 44 *percent* in top-tier law schools, according to *BusinessWeek.*[2] The reason for the spread is that many women don't feel that business really makes a difference in the world: "Many women don't even consider careers in business and feel more attracted to medical and law schools, which have successfully marketed themselves as places to pursue more service-oriented careers," according to Jeanne M. Wilt, assistant dean for admissions and career development at Michigan, quoted in *Business-Week.* Corporate integrity in this century has reached all-time lows, a fact that can conceivably turn off socially conscientious women. But no one is forcing you to seek positions with socially irresponsible or negligent companies. It is another one of the choices you need to make in your career.

In the 1980s, if you went to law school you practiced law. Today's female law school graduates parlay their degree into all professional fields and most often successfully. You don't need an MBA or a professional or law degree to succeed. But it helps, if for no other reason than it provides you with bona fide credibility. How you give meaning to those degrees is entirely up to you.

The real story, though, is in our numbers and how we fare in the overall management picture. We are disappointed to see the slow progress of women at the top. Gen Xers and Yers need to swell the pipeline so when they are ready, the sheer numbers of talented women available for the top slots will ensure their selection.

On the good news side—more women are listed as corporate officers than ever before, and the critical mass is denser. Women are advancing in line positions, which, of course, is the feeding ground for the executive floor. But still almost 20 percent of Fortune 500 companies, 90 of them, don't have any female corporate officers at all; although that shows some progress from five years before when 115 companies had no women officers, the going is rather slow.[3] Salary studies mirror the power positions as well.

Catalyst's study found that 2,140 women are among the 13,673 corporate officers in the nation's 500 largest companies, 15.7 percent, up from 12.5 percent in 2000, and 11.9 percent in 1999. Ten percent, or fifty of the Fortune 500 companies have women holding a quarter or more of the corporate officer titles, twice the number since 1995, when

Catalyst began measuring this data. Even more promising, four companies have reached more than 40 percent women corporate officers: Ikon Office Solutions, SLM Holdings, PacifiCare Health Systems, and Nordstrom. "In the race for talent, some companies are starting to get it. It's certainly not time to declare victory and go home. But over time, these small, incremental increases add up to real change," said Sheila Wellington, president of Catalyst.[4]

But we don't seem to get that much further ahead in the CEO positions themselves. We always have between two and six. Sometimes the woman is ousted like Jill Barad, former CEO of Mattel; sometimes a woman executive falls off the list of female CEOs of Fortune 500 companies, like Golden West Financial Corp.'s CEO Marion Sandler (and in this case, comes back on). Cinda Hallman, CEO of Spherion, the provider of temporary and permanent personnel, made the list in 2000, dropped off in 2001 but made the Fortune 1000 in 2002 after effective streamlining and cost-cutting operations. For the time being, we have reached a position of having six CEOs, but that hold is tenuous. At the helm of companies in the Fortune 500, we find Carleton (Carly) Fiorina at Hewlett-Packard, Andrea Jung at Avon Products, Marion Sandler at Golden West Financial, Marce Fuller at Mirant, and now, finally, Anne Mulcahy at Xerox and Patricia Russo at Lucent.

We have fared a little bit better in the positions that lead to CEO. In 2002, women represented 9.9 percent of "clout" titles, compared with 7.9 percent the year before, and 1.9 percent in 1995. Clout titles, the positions that wield the most policy-making power, include chief executive officer, chairman, vice chairman, president, chief financial officer, chief operating officer, senior executive vice president, and executive vice president.

Catalyst has also projected that if women—who comprise close to half of today's workforce—continue to make progress at the same rate, it will take twenty years for them to crack the one-quarter mark, to hold 27.4 percent of corporate officer positions. That's a lot to think about. If the prediction is correct, that would not be much progress after so long and so much hard work. On the other hand, how many of us are willing to make the necessary sacrifices to change the status quo? These are heady choices, and many women have made conscious decisions not to take the challenge in order to protect a quality of life or raise a family. Deciding to pursue a senior management position remains a matter of personal choice and commitment, even if we break through the barriers.

"But it still seems doubtful," Gail Collins believes, "that women will soon reach full equality. At the present rate, it will be 2270 before women are as likely as men to become top managers in corporations and 2500 before there is gender parity in Congress."[5] Yikes. And if we take into consideration that the years 2001–2005 may be dead in the water for women's advancement, we truly are looking at life just after the middle ages for the foreseeable future.

General Electric is the quintessential example of an ol' boy establishment. Before Jeff Immelt took over the top position, rumors abounded about who would become Jack Welch's successor as chief executive of the company. Although minorities, including women, blacks, Latinos, and Asians make up 40 percent of the domestic workforce, there was only one black in the exalted group of couldbes and no women, Latinos, or Asians. And of the corporate officers at GE in total, only 6.4 percent are women, as compared with the 11.9 percent average of the companies researched by Catalyst.[6]

GE is not alone. If we check all the Fortune, Forbes, or BusinessWeek Top 500 lists we find similar numbers. The few women in top posts, or the second or third top posts, are already well known. There are no hidden trump cards waiting for a spot. No matter how diversified companies are, they don't ask the recruiters to find them a woman to wear the crown. So if one of the three top men in contention for the CEO spot is chosen, the other two take the top slot at other companies. Headhunters seek them out and hunt them down. Just being known as a contender gets the loser a good spot.

Women haven't even begun to play in that league. If there is one of us, that's it, except perhaps at Hewlett-Packard, when Carly battled it out with Ann Livermore for the top position. And when women CEOs leave their companies, men usually replace them, particularly if women leave following disappointing earnings. The message is that if things turn bad with a woman at the helm, let's go back to the comfort zone. In 1999–2000, we saw similar awkward departures by Rebecca Marx at Azurix and Jill Barad at Mattel. In both cases, men replaced the women and the companies experienced some restructuring. Mattel is still not out of its doldrums and Enron, Azurix mother company is, well, worthy of a book or more on its own.

In all fairness, GE at least has made some effort, albeit slim, to increase diversification. According to Williams Walsh, author of a *New York Times* article about GE's CEO succession plan, diversity had been on the corporate agenda for thirty years. GE's efforts to retain women and minorities have intensified in recent years. Welch made diversity a top priority in his last year not necessarily because he felt this from his core but because he believed it was a bottom-line necessity. Hypothetically.

GE has always been known as a tough culture to penetrate. Welch was a strong leader with a firm commitment to earnings and growth, something for which his shareholders had always been thankful. However, this same corporate mission had some in the company wondering if diversity would fit with this conviction. Diversity and growth/earnings are not mutually exclusive if the company truly seeks the best and the brightest around the world. There are a lot of women out there who are top-notch and who would be a good addition to any corporation. But we all also know some sacrifices must be made, either in how we move along in our personal lives or with whom we choose to move along. As Karen Nelson, former GE Medical Systems marketing manager, stated in the *New York Times* article cited in the last paragraph: "Frankly, I don't know how to begin to change the GE culture. All we were saying was, 'Let's level the playing field.' Now, do we really want to say, 'We have to change the game altogether'?"[7]

Companies like GE are at least making the effort by diversifying their boards with, for example, Andrea Jung, CEO of Avon, and Ann Fudge, EVP of Kraft Foods. Both are minority women. Any empowerment of women in the corporation or diversity initiative is a start in the right direction and shows that there is some corporate conscience. However, as Williams Walsh clearly predicted, it didn't make much difference in the selection of Jack Welch's successor.

Even in this new millennium, the same concerns that have permeated the corporate world for the last twenty years still prevail: many male middle managers are often frightened of women. It is not just their own survival in the company at stake, but in the larger sense, it is their whole sense of worth and identity. "Men can feel very threatened," cautioned Chickie Bucco.

Young women in the workforce today need to understand that in terms of power positions we are sorely behind, despite the progress that men love to flaunt. To reiterate, one Carly Fiorina does not mean that any woman can get to the top. And if parity has been hard to achieve in power stats and positions, it has been even more elusive in compensation. No matter how hard we work or how high we go, we never get where the boys are. And that, for those old enough to remember, is not Fort Lauderdale, Florida, during spring break.

The General Accounting Office (GAO) published results in June 2002[8] from a study comparing how much a woman earns for each dollar earned by a man:

Sector	1995	2000	Change
Entertainment and recreation	83 cents	62 cents	− 21 cents
Communications	86	73	− 13
Finance, insurance, and real estate	76	68	− 8
Business services and repairs	82	76	− 6
Other professional services	88	83	− 5
Retail trade	69	65	− 4
Professional medical services	90	88	− 2
Public administration	80	83	+ 3
Hospital and medical services	80	85	+ 5
Education	86	91	+ 5

The report, commissioned by Representatives Carolyn Maloney (D-NY) and John Dingell (D-Mich.), reveals that we continue to be "under-represented in senior management positions in virtually every professional field. And although women have made steady improvements in the workplace as a whole, earning 76 cents for every dollar that a man takes home, the data clearly show that progress is stalled for women in management positions. In short, the glass ceiling has hardened, rather than shattered, since 1995."[9]

Almost any woman in business could have saved the government a lot of money offering the same information and some upsetting stories as accompaniment. Without sounding like an alarmist, those are the facts. And every woman in business, from entry level through management, has to know this. She has to know this so she won't be surprised, or hurt, by thinking there is something wrong with her. She has to know this so she can be prepared. Those Boy Scouts beat us to that motto, too.

In a report released a few months prior to the Dingell-Maloney report, the Committee of 200, a "20-year-old network of top women entrepreneurs and corporate leaders," published its first Business Leadership Index. "It showed how businesswomen fared in relation to men on a 10-point scale, with 10 representing parity with men. In an aggregate of 10 separate benchmarks, women scored an overall 3.95."[10]

The Business Leadership study also predicted how long it would take women to reach parity with men in areas of board membership in the Fortune 500, access to venture-capital funding, enrollment in graduate business programs, and gender pay. Venture-capital funding obtained a low score, as did corporate officer positions at Fortune 500 companies: "Women will reach only the halfway mark on the journey to parity between 2018 and 2020, the study predicts." Even wage parity will take about thirty years. The Business Leadership study agrees with the *BusinessWeek* report on the Catalyst Survey on women and the MBA cited earlier in this chapter: "Business schools need to be more aggressive in recruiting women and companies should encourage their female employees to pursue these credentials that often open doors to lucrative careers."[11]

Not to be undone, the IRS also conducted a study and discovered that "as salary grows, so does a gender gap: women may be bringing home larger paychecks, but when it comes to earning the really serious money—wages of $1 million or more—men far outnumber them, as they did a generation ago."[12]

In fact, in 1998, 43,662 men earned at least $1 million compared with 3,253 women. And even then, a man earned $2.41 million to the woman's $2.27. In the $500,000–$1 million category, men outnumbered women ten to one, but the women had slightly higher averages at $670,000 versus $668,000 for the men. Women are way out front at the $20,000–$25,000 level, though.

Without a doubt, the disparity is much higher at the top. While men are accepting women more and more in middle management, they still hold the very top for themselves. As more women stay the course and move up the ranks, the comparisons should eventually become more balanced. But we are looking at decades before we come close to those stellar tippy-top numbers. With larger numbers we may at some point be able to create an equal but separate dominance in the CEO pinnacle spot, and the more we help each other, the faster we will get there. Young women entering the workforce today will have a shot at parity, if all goes as planned. But as the lottery slogan goes, "You've got to be in it to win it."

Clustering also exists in a big way. Although we have made ample progress, we are growing our traditional professions and barely dipping our toes in those that have never invited us in to begin with. According to the U.S. Department of Labor, we hold the following percentages in these occupations:

Engineers	9.9%
Architects	23.5
Lawyers	29.6
Math and computer scientists	31.4

Writers, artists, entertainers, and athletes	50.0
Financial managers	50.1
Economists	53.3
Sales workers, retail and personal services	63.5
Social workers	72.4
Administrative support and clerical	79.0

And, although this book is about how women should thrive in the workplace, we are also struggling to attain top-level political positions in this country. Women make up 52 percent of the population. We outvote men and now run approximately 40 percent of small businesses in the United States, but in the 2003 Congress, and top elected positions, we only have

13 percent of the U.S. Senate (13 women)

22 percent of the U.S. Supreme Court (2)

28.5 percent of the U.S. Cabinet (4 of 14)

13.8 percent of the U.S. House (59)

12 percent of U.S. governors (6)

20.6 percent of federal judges (332)[13]

Men also outnumber women in the general top ranks of Washington, according to *BusinessWeek*.[14] At a four to one ratio, "of federal jobs paying $120,000 or more, roughly 12,000 are held by men, 3,000 by women. Except in the Office of the U.S. Trade Representative (USTR) where eight of the 15 assistant trade reps—top staff at most negotiating tables—are female, and two of the four deputy and associate trade reps are women."

There are currently ten female heads of state or government throughout the world and twenty-eight who previously ran their countries. But, according to Lori Lessner, from the *Miami Herald*'s Washington Bureau, women in the United States have the same problems in politics as they do in the workplace: not enough support and/or commitment from other women: "They say that unless more women put politics at the center of their lives—recruiting and supporting one another as they pursue political power—the country will continue to be shaped without women at the helm."[15] Emily's List (the acronym for Early Money Is Like Yeast—i.e., to bring in the "dough") is working hard to rectify the support system by forming a political network to support women candidates. The group was created to support pro-choice women candidates, but the mandate has expanded to champion women candidates for their pledge to bring about the necessary change to improve women's lot overall.

There still needs to be a considerable change in mind-set. A national survey, according to Lessner's article, has found that "both male and female voters still prefer a man to a woman for offices such as governor, attorney general and president." And, by and large, both male and female employees expect to see a man at the helm of a corporation, private business, or law firm. Probably the only places where a woman is expected to be found is as a mother, nurse, or teacher. New century, same old mind-set.

The glass ceiling is not just for old-timers. It isn't only in business. And it isn't history. It would have been nice to say it was a twentieth-century phenomenon. It would make a nice memoir. We speak about the glass ceiling as indicative of a time that occurred decades ago. We now find it has hardened in many spots. We also have sore heads from constantly bumping up against it. And now, as Chickie Bucco notes, "there is even a sticky floor. There is still so far to go for women."

Equality 2020,[16] a Web site "focused on the advancements and setbacks in achieving full equality for women," compiled the following "fast facts" to heighten women's awareness about where we stand in business, government, the media, and law:

- Women scientists earn nearly one-third less than their male counterparts.
- Women in law remain underrepresented in positions of greatest status, influence, and economic reward.
- Men working in Congress hold more executive and policy positions, while women hold more midlevel and support positions.
- Men working in Congress earn higher salaries than females in the chief of staff position and the press secretary position.
- Women are only 9 percent of the board members in major media, telecom, and e-companies, and are only 13 percent of top executives.
- Women managers in finance earn 76 cents for every dollar earned by male managers.
- Women are only 11 percent of guests on the Sunday morning talk shows, limiting their access to the power of agenda-setting television programs in shaping elite and public opinion.
- Large majorities of women cite several barriers to women's advancement in their firms, whereas most men cite only women's commitment to family or lack of experience as barriers.

And while we are compiling and digesting the statistics that matter most to us, two more lists deserve scrutiny on the part of any job-searching or job-changing woman. The first and most important for us is the Top 25 Companies list for Executive Women, compiled annually by the NAFE—National Association of Female Executives. After careful research and study, the NAFE found that the following companies are the most hospitable for executive women (*executive* in this case means any woman with the ambition, the drive, the desire, and the intention to get to that corner office): Avon, Liz Claiborne, Aetna, Allstate, CIGNA, Fannie Mae, Lincoln Financial, The Phoenix Companies, Principal Financial, Prudential, Sallie Mae, State Street, TIAA-CREF, Washington Mutual, Federated, Sears, SBC Communications, Hewlett-Packard, IBM, The New York Times Company, Scholastic, Con-Ed, Merck, WellPoint, Advantica.[17]

The last list determines the states where we live that are the most welcoming. The Institute for Women's Policy Research, a Washington, D.C.–based nonprofit organization compared women's employment and earnings opportunities across the United States in terms of overall jobs, wage parity, and managerial and professional positions. According to the research,

> Women's participation in managerial and professional jobs has been growing since 1994 . . . but female managers are unlikely to earn to-dollar in such positions. The District of Columbia ranks No. 1 in the survey, with 48 percent of its working women occupying professional and managerial jobs, compared with a national average of 32.2 percent. Idaho is ranked last among the states. . . . Taking into account all the factors in IWPR's Employment and Earnings Index, the District of Columbia, Maryland, Alaska, Minnesota and Colorado were ranked the highest. The states that ranked the lowest were West Virginia, Louisiana, Mississippi, Wyoming and Arkansas.[18]

Find a company that is happy to have found you. Not all companies, as we have seen, are women-friendly. "If you're at a firm that's not interested in creating a culture where you can grow, cut out of there fast. I always tell women: 'Don't sit around and complain. Find a place that wants you,'" says Anne Tatlock, chairman of Fiduciary Trust.[19] That is the quintessential bottom line for a woman.

NOTES

1. Mary Williams Walsh, "Number of Women in Upper Ranks Rises a Bit," *New York Times,* November 19, 2002.

2. Jennifer Reingold, "It's Still a Guy Thing," *BusinessWeek,* May 22, 2000, p. 58.

3. Catalyst 2000 Census of Women Corporate Officers and Top Earners, data from Catalyst Survey "Women and the MBA: Gateway to Opportunity," November 2000.

4. Catalyst Survey of Executive and High-earning Corporate Women, November 2002.

5. Gail Collins, "Women, 'A Social Glacier Roars,' *The New York Times Magazine* May 16, 1999.

6. Mary Williams Walsh, "Where G.E. Falls Short: Diversity at the Top," *New York Times,* September 3, 2000.

7. Ibid.

8. These data are from the Dingell-Maloney Report published by the General Accounting Office, commissioned by Representatives John Dingell (D-MI) and Carolyn Maloney (D-NY), reprinted in *BusinessWeek,* June 24, 2002. p. 151.

9. Congresswoman Carolyn Maloney press release, January 24, 2002: "The Dingell-Maloney Report: A New Look through the glass ceiling shows the glass ceiling hardened, rather than shattered, after 1995."

10. Laura Koss-Feder, "Study Finds Wage Gap Is Just the Beginning," *Women's eNews,* April 16, 2002.

11. Catalyst Survey, "Women and the MBA: Gateway to Opportunity," May 2000.

12. David Cay Johnston, "As Salary Grows, So Does a Gender Gap," *New York Times,* May 12, 2002.

13. The figures were obtained from www.gendergap.com, November 2002.

14. Paul Magnusson, "In the Trade War Trenches: Women," *BusinessWeek,* February 25, 2002.

15. Lori Lessner, "Women Lacking in Top-level Political Positions," *Miami Herald,* December 1, 1999.

16. www.equality2020.org

17. *Executive Female Magazine,* February 2001.

18. "Best States for Women: Women's Quest for Economic Parity with Men Progresses More in Some States Than Others, Study Finds," *CNN/Money, CNN.com,* November 19, 2002. Original study from Institute for Women's Policy Research, "The Status of Women in the States," Washington, D.C.

19. Quoted in Melinda Ligos, "Escape Route from Sexist Attitudes on Wall St.," *New York Times,* May 30, 2001.

EPILOGUE

It is never too late to be what you might have been.
—George Eliot

The process is simple. To lose weight, eat less and exercise more. To succeed, believe in yourself, create alignment, ask questions, and focus. Most of all, learn to laugh at yourself. You may not make it to CEO, but you can work toward that goal. You may also never be a size 4 if you are 5′9″ but you wouldn't want to give up and hide in the size 18s, would you?

Be kind to yourself. And trust yourself. Your instincts are good, your intuition is right on. Don't be afraid to make mistakes. Believe in you and the good you can leave behind. And while you are doing that, have fun! And see to it that those around you have fun, too. Find the passion in what you are doing. If it isn't fun and you don't love it, look elsewhere. But remember, knowledge *is* power. Read everything you can get your hands on and always be one step ahead of your clients, your boss, and your colleagues. The more you know, the better decisions you will make and the more you will believe in your own abilities. As the late, great tennis player, Arthur Ashe said, "One important key to success is self-confidence. An important key to self-confidence is preparation."

Wherever you are in your career, make an effort to share your stories and your knowledge with a younger generation of women, of whatever age. If we all don't start to pick up the slack in mentoring or role modeling or just teaching the ropes, we stand a good chance of losing ground when and if it behooves men to try and take it away from us in the future. It is our responsibility to see that newer generations of women get the mentoring they will need. There are such things as scapegoats, and equality falls by the wayside when few jobs are available; the old mind-set of men needing jobs and the money to raise a family is barely subliminal.

Find your own road. The guidelines provided throughout the book encapsulate what all the women I spoke with have told me. The advice given isn't a strategy, or a daily plan, or a manual. It is what your role model would want you to know. It is how you should be bringing up your daughter or your niece, or your employee. It is how you should be thinking about yourself and how you manage your career. I hope our examples, our stories, will give future generations the needed affirmation to succeed. Because as we all know: "I'm good enough, I'm smart enough, and doggone it, people like me."[1]

NOTE

1. Stuart Smalley (aka Al Franken).

BIBLIOGRAPHY

Cain, Madelyn. *The Childless Revolution: What it Means to Be Childless Today.* New York: Perseus, 2001.

Covey, Stephen R. *The 7 Habits of Highly Effective People.* New York: Fireside, 1990.

Estrich, Susan. *Sex and Power.* New York: Riverhead, 2001.

Faludi, Susan. *Backlash: The Undeclared War against American Women.* New York: Crown, 1991.

Hennig, Margaret, and Anne Jardim. *The Managerial Woman.* New York: Pocket Books, 1978.

Hewlett, Sylvia Ann. *Creating a Life: Professional Women and the Quest for Children.* New York: Talk Miramax Books, 2002.

Lehan Harragan, Betty. *Games Mother Never Taught You.* New York: Warner Books, 1978.

Roth Madden, Tara. *Women vs. Women, the Uncivil Business War.* New York: Amacom, 1987.

Sheehy, Gail. *Pathfinders.* New York: William Morrow & Company, 1981.

Wellington, Sheila, et al. *Be Your Own Mentor: Strategies from Top Women on the Secrets of Success.* New York: Random House, 2001.

Wiesen Cook, Blanche. *Eleanor Roosevelt: Volume 2: 1933–1938.* New York: Viking, 1999.

Zientara, Marguerite. *Women, Technology and Power: Ten Stars and the History They Made.* New York: Amacom, 1987.

INDEX

About the Author

DIANE SMALLEN-GROB is a full-time writer.